Dear God, My Life Is In Jeopardy

Tom Covino

TRILOGY
A WHOLLY OWNED SUBSIDIARY OF **TBN**
PROFESSIONAL PUBLISHING MEETS POWERFUL PROMOTION

Trilogy Christian Publishers

A Wholly Owned Subsidiary of Trinity Broadcasting Network

2442 Michelle Drive

Tustin, CA 92780

Copyright © 2024 by Tom Covino

All Scripture quotations are taken from the ESV® Bible (The Holy Bible, English Standard Version®), copyright © 2001 by Crossway Bibles, a publishing ministry of Good News Publishers. Used by permission. All rights reserved.

All rights reserved, including the right to reproduce this book or portions thereof in any form whatsoever.

For information, address Trilogy Christian Publishing

Rights Department, 2442 Michelle Drive, Tustin, Ca 92780.

Trilogy Christian Publishing/TBN and colophon are trademarks of Trinity Broadcasting Network.

For information about special discounts for bulk purchases, please contact Trilogy Christian Publishing.

Trilogy Disclaimer: The views and content expressed in this book are those of the author and may not necessarily reflect the views and doctrine of Trilogy Christian Publishing or the Trinity Broadcasting Network.

10 9 8 7 6 5 4 3 2 1

Library of Congress Cataloging-in-Publication Data is available.

ISBN 979-8-89041-704-6

ISBN 979-8-89041-705-3 (ebook)

"I can't recall a book that affected me so much. From suspenseful and gripping, from Jeopardy to the final courtroom, this book shook me to the core."

-Maureen in Florida

Dedication

The inspiration for writing this book comes from God's grace, love, and providential care as they collided one night with the heart of one Hollywood actress appearing as a guest on the Stephen Colbert late-night talk show. The result was a great shout to God and the rest of the world, watching that night for the relief of her greatest fear.

Table of Contents

Dedication IV
Part 1: The Game 1
Chapter 1: Let's Play Jeopardy 1
Chapter 2: Intermission 14
Chapter 3: Final Jeopardy 23
Connecting "Spiritual Dots" 42
Part 2: It Is Not A Game 48
The Seven Doors of Death 48
A Word from the Illustrator, Jason Roberts 119

Part 1: The Game

Chapter 1: Let's Play Jeopardy

E. D. Raines, *Jeopardy!*'s new game show host, gathered the studio audience together for one last prep talk. This was no regular group of people. Sitting in tonight's seats were some of the most famous celebrities of the last forty years.

The elite singers, actors, and athletes who have been filtering through our television sets were now ready to participate in one of the most recognized shows of all time.

The night's contestant was Evelyn Dawson, a retired business executive, married to her high-school sweetheart, Jeff, and mother to two beautiful daughters: Victoria, twenty-seven, and Adeline, twenty-five.

Just prior to being called out to the stage, Evelyn looked out into the audience, catching a quick glimpse of two mega stars, Lady Gaga and Bradley Cooper. Starstruck, she took a deep breath, wondering to herself how she got to be on a show that she'd watched most of her adult life.

Evelyn thought it was a bit strange to be the only contestant on a show that typically had three and wondered why the studio audience was filled with the very best entertainers instead of a regular crowd; nevertheless, she was excited to play.

Prior to the game beginning, the producer took her aside,

telling her that this was a new type of *Jeopardy!* game that featured the entertainers as sort of co-show hosts, asking most of the questions, while E. D. would act as a surrogate armchair quarterback.

In this new generation, gone were the days of the moderator asking questions of three brainiacs from a non-confrontational distance; instead, a new and personal version would be the path that placed both E. D. and Evelyn comfortably sitting next to each other on matching sofas.

With many butterflies swirling around inside of her, Evelyn suddenly felt extremely uncomfortable. She couldn't find Jeff or the girls.

Final Instructions to the Stars

"Okay, gang," said E. D. "Remember what I've told you from the very beginning of rehearsals; keep your earpieces in at all times. There will be a ten-second delay from our set to the people watching from home in case we need to ad-lib on the fly. If and when I call your name, please make sure to stand and hold up your question-and-answer card for Evelyn and the millions of fans watching at home to see. Remember, although you are the best performers in the world, you will have to convey your message and emotions without saying a word—style and emotion matter. Please smile and act with the greatest of convictions. If I see that you are going a bit overboard, I'll raise my left index finger, indicating that I want you to wrap it up. Adele, Jennifer Lopez, Drake, Adam Levine, Blake Shelton, Leonardo DiCaprio, Robert Downey Jr., Will Smith, Jennifer Lawrence, Scarlett Johansson, Emma Stone, Emma Watson, Charlize Theron, Morgan Freeman, Ryan Gosling, and Julia Roberts…thank you all for your auditions; they were fantastic as usual. We won't need you for this particular game, but we expect to use you in the near future. However, we will need you to participate by just being in the audience tonight. For those who do have roles for Evelyn's game, one last thing: I'm passing out the entire script of questions for you to see. On it are the names of each actor, singer, or athlete and their respective topic questions, so there should be no confusion."

Then, he said, "Everyone, take your places; ten seconds to showtime!"

As *Jeopardy!*'s theme song began to play, E. D. walked out to the stage to a resounding round of applause. At the exact same moment, there was a huge thud backstage, like something had just fallen to the ground. Never one to be distracted, E. D. whispered into everyone's earpieces, "Lights, camera, action!"

The Game Begins

"Good evening, everyone, and welcome to *Jeopardy!* Before we meet our first contestant, can we have a moment of silence for the late great Alex Trebek, 1940–2020? We will miss him terribly. And now, it's my pleasure to introduce Evelyn Dawson to the show."

As she walked out to meet E. D., Evelyn couldn't resist looking out into the audience. She saw Tom Hanks, LeBron James, and Oprah Winfrey all clapping. Evelyn knew that the claps were meant as an approval of the show and not necessarily toward her, but she couldn't help but get caught up in the moment, feeling like, for one brief moment, she was the star.

As Evelyn sat down next to E. D., she quickly noticed that it was considerably colder than backstage. E. D., always prepared, picked up a blanket and draped it around Evelyn's shoulders, whispering, "It's a bit chilly in here. Evelyn, how are you today?"

"Well, Ed, I have to admit I'm a little more nervous than usual. I've never been on this or any stage before, so I'm not sure what to expect."

"That's okay, Evelyn; the stars you see sitting in our audience are nervous, too. It's their first time on this show as well. And if you don't mind, I'd love it if you call me E. D."

Then, E. D. asked, "Tell us something about yourself."

"Well, I've been married to a wonderful man named Jeff for the past twenty-five years. I'm a mother of two precious girls, Victoria and Adeline, who seem to be playing some trick on me because I lost track of them only a few minutes before the show began."

"No worries, Evelyn, they have special seating backstage. I can assure you they're doing just fine."

Evelyn continued feeling more at ease. "I've been in the banking business most of my life. I love all sports, watching movies with my husband, and going to music concerts, especially with the girls. I also get to travel to other countries to discuss the various types of currency and how it affects the economy. You know, a banking thing."

"Well, speaking of banking," said E. D. "Each question in round one is going to be worth $2,500. Evelyn, we don't have our typical columns of categories like before when Alex was hosting the show. Instead, one of our stars seated in the audience will stand up while holding a card with the category and question on one side and the answer on the back. Before you were chosen to be on the show, all potential contestants filled out a deeper, more extensive questionnaire about themselves. We, in turn, will be asking questions based on our knowledge of you and your knowledge about the many stars sitting in the audience right in front of you."

"Evelyn Dawson, let's play *Jeopardy!*"

Question 1

With great excitement, E. D. said, "Sitting in the audience is a well-known English pop rock band that became famous in the United States during the 'new wave' craze. Please welcome the lead singer for the 1980s group Tears For Fears, Curt Smith."

Curt held up a sign that read, "Hi, Evelyn. This is a two-part question, each worth $2,500, so you can start your game by winning a potential $5,000. One of our hit songs began with the word 'welcome,' do you recall what this welcome was all about?"

"Absolutely!" said Evelyn, "What is 'to your life'?"

Before Curt could respond, E. D. jumped in, saying, "That's correct!" Though it startled Evelyn, she was excited to hear the second part of the question. The card read, "What is the name of that song?"

Evelyn had heard that song thousands of times growing up in the Northeast during the early '80s. She had always believed that "Welcome to Your Life" was actually the name of the song. She began to fidget in her chair as she mouthed the rest of the song while recalling it in her head.

E. D. looked at Evelyn and asked, "Would you like Curt to give you some extra help?"

"Is that allowed?" she asked.

"Stars, what do you say?" asked E. D.

The cast from the hit show *This Is Us* all stood up together with their thumbs in the air, with Mandy Moore leading the way as she held up a sign that read, "Evelyn, when E. D. speaks, everyone listens."

"Well then," said Evelyn, looking at Mandy. "Sounds good to me. Yes, E. D., I would love some help."

Curt and the group Tears For Fears began playing the instrumental part of the song only. It was exhilaratingly effective. Evelyn began tapping her feet in rhythm to the beat.

Suddenly, Evelyn jumped into the air, shouting, "Everybody Wants to Rule the World."

The look on E. D.'s face said it all, "You just won $5,000. How does that feel?"

"It's surreal, E. D.," Evelyn said, "I've never made that much money in such a short period of time, and I work in a bank."

A big laugh was heard from all the stars, making Evelyn feel that much more comfortable.

Evelyn looked out at the crowd of stars. She caught a glimpse of her daughter Adeline's heartthrob Nick Jonas, standing there clapping alongside singer Kelly Clarkson, song coach from the hit show *The Voice*.

In all of the excitement, E. D. encouraged Evelyn to sit back down next to him as he said, "Evelyn, we have a long way to go in our game. I want to remind you that if your total winnings are in the black and not in the red at the end of the show, you win!"

Question 2

E. D. looked out into the audience and shouted similarly to the way they do in the hit game show *The Price Is Right*, "Paul McCartney and Billy Joel, please stand up!"

Billy Joel stood up, holding a card that had a picture of three people and an unknown bartender sitting together, all having a drink.

Paul McCartney, the Beatle of all Beatles, stood up next to Billy Joel with his card that read, "Eleanor Rigby."

Together, like at the Oscars, they flipped their cards over simultaneously, which read, "Evelyn, what does the picture of people sitting together with a bartender and the song 'Eleanor Rigby' have in common?"

During the interview process, E. D. told each finalist that it was important to be able to think quickly on their feet and to be able to entertain the people at home while looking at their favorite childhood heroes. In addition, one of the critical aspects of the interview process in selecting a contestant was giving each of them a catchphrase to remember.

"You're only going to play this game once!"

Evelyn, remembering the catchphrase, teased both Joel and McCartney on one of the most-watched television shows of all time, saying, "Well, guys, I could say… Something about Father Mckenzie [looking at McCartney] or about the waitress practicing politics [catching eyes with Billy], but how about I just say, 'What is 'being alone''?"

An anticipated hush came over the crowd while E. D. looked over at the judges for the verdict. While waiting for them to respond, McCartney quickly held up a second sign that read, "All the lonely people, where do they all come from?"

"*Yes*! We will accept it," said E. D., explaining to Evelyn that the judges were looking for the word "loneliness" or any form of the word. "Congratulations, Evelyn, that's another $2,500, bringing your total to $7,500! You're doing great."

Question 3

Prior to the show's beginning, as the entertainers were reading over their scripts, an uneasy feeling came over them. They disputed directly with E. D. as to whether question number 3 was appropriate to ask in light of its sensitive nature.

When they unanimously decided that they wouldn't participate, E. D. went to the producers of the show to get their opinion. They and the writers decided on an effective way of asking Evelyn a question that would mitigate all her personal feelings while at the same time having an honorable effect on both the stars participating and the fans watching from home.

E. D. whispered into the earpiece of actor Matthew McConaughey, "I need you to stand up and be a professional!"

Matthew stood up and walked to the stage, handing Evelyn an envelope, and then proceeded to sit back down in protest. It read, "As you can see, we have left five empty seats in the front row as a reminder of some wonderful people who have left us way too soon. Can you match the correct name with these clues? Each answer is worth $1,000, for a potential of another $5,000."

These read: "*I Want to Be a Millionaire*," "The *Black Panther*," "Right-Wing Radio Host," "*Dear Basketball*," and "*Good Morning, Vietnam*."

Evelyn looked at the empty seats. Tears filled her eyes as she began to recall some of the names that matched each phrase. Before answering the question, Evelyn looked directly into the eyes of Matthew McConaughey, sitting just off to the right, and said, "Of all the movies you've ever made, *Contact* is my favorite. I've watched it many, many times."

Matthew nodded in appreciation.

Evelyn knew she had to be brave while at the same time showing respect as she gave her answers.

"My first answer is Kobe Bryant for *Dear Basketball*, and if I may say, E. D., I am still horrified at the thought that Kobe is no longer with us. What happened was so tragic that I'm not sure any of us will ever get over it entirely. My next answer is Regis Philbin with the show *I Want to Be a Millionaire*. My husband, Jeff, and I loved to watch this with the kids. Regis was fantastic. My third answer is, I believe, it's Rush Limbaugh as the conservative radio host."

Evelyn looked over at E. D., knowing of the sensitive nature of

Mr. Limbaugh's political stance but wanting to say something.

With a small nod from E. D., Evelyn said, "Like him or not, he took a stand, but I guess it doesn't matter anymore. My fourth answer is… E. D., it pains me to even say the next name. I can picture his face like he's almost sitting next to me. He made me laugh so much over my lifetime and cry, too. He was amazing in *Dead Poets Society* and *Good Will Hunting*, and I had almost forgotten about *Good Morning, Vietnam*. When I think of Robin Williams, I'll always smile, but I was horrified when I heard he took his own life."

The camera panned around the theater as all the iconic figures gasped in unison.

E. D. stepped in, attempting to soften the blow. "Don't worry, Evelyn, I'm pretty sure that Robin is making everyone laugh up in heaven."

Evelyn struggled with "The *Black Panther*."

"Both of my daughters enjoy all of the Marvel movies; together, we've seen this one at least three times. I can see his face. He fought with the guy who played Creed… Ah, oh yeah, Michael B. Jordan."

E. D. asked, "Is that your guess?"

"No!" Evelyn shot back. "No, he was the challenger in the fight. I have it! The answer is 'Chadwick Boseman.'"

As soon as she said his name, it hit Evelyn and everyone else that Chadwick Boseman was only forty-three years old when he died. As Evelyn looked into the audience, she saw how the death of one actor affected all the other actors who knew him. Evelyn caught a glimpse of Denzel Washington with his head down while others let their tears roll down their cheeks.

E. D. knew that as hard as it was to put such a question in a gameshow like the old *Jeopardy!*, the new and improved version had to hit the emotional heartstrings of everyone involved. And with that, E. D. yelled out, "Evelyn Dawson, you just won $5,000 more; you got all five answers right. You now have a total of $12,500. I want to thank Matthew McConaughey for asking you a very difficult question. Now, will everyone please take a look up at the screen in front of you?"

There he was, Kobe Bryant, holding up an Oscar for his animated film *Dear Basketball*. Collectively, everyone stood up and cheered wildly, holding up signs saying, "Mamba rules! And Mamba lives!"

Question 4

"Evelyn, there will be one more question before we take a short break. After that, we will play Double Jeopardy, where the dollar amounts are doubled and the questions more difficult."

E. D. looked at Evelyn, sizing her up, when he said, "Before you ask me the question that I can see is burning in your heart, the answer is yes, we still have the Daily Doubles!"

"You must have been reading my mind, E. D.," Evelyn responded. "That's exactly what I was thinking." Two seconds later, a newly devised "Daily Double" sound was heard. It was this high-pitched sound of "He-He."

"E. D.," said Evelyn, "was that Michael Jackson's 'He-He' or someone else's?"

E. D. responded, "There's only one man who was able to make a sound like that, other than perhaps the Bee Gees."

The crowd laughed.

"Yes, it's the one and only Michael Jackson."

The camera caught a glimpse of a few athletic GOATs in the room: Chicago Bulls' Michael Jordan, arguably the NBA's greatest player to ever put on a jersey; current NFL GOAT quarterback Tom Brady, who just happened to be sitting next to Tiger Woods, and the greatest known swimmer, Michael Phelps.

The GOATs turned toward the back of the room, only to see the back of the greatest modern entertainer of all time. Michael was in all black, wearing his famous shiny silver glove on his left hand.

"Wait a minute. Do you know how many Chicago Bulls games I've seen? Michael Jordan is in the audience?" she said with enormous excitement. "E. D., how did you know that I loved all these great athletes? I mean, I love golf and Tiger Woods. My husband Jeff and I also love watching the NFL. I have to admit, I'm more of an Aaron Rogers fan, but Tom Brady is the GOAT for sure. As for Michael Phelps, watching him win all those gold medals was amazing."

Evelyn got so caught up in the moment of seeing her favorite athletes that she almost forgot about the Daily Double. And then it hit her…

"Hold on, E. D., that can't be Michael Jackson. He's been gone for a while now."

The drumbeat to one of Michael's greatest songs began to play. Evelyn knew it by the third note; it was "Billie Jean." Evelyn could see Michael's feet stepping to the music. Looking at E. D., Evelyn asked, "Is that really Michael or some impersonating actor they brought in from the street?"

E. D. replied, "Watch and see."

Some of the actors in the front row had just caught up to what was going on; they began standing, waiting for Michael to make a move. Would he moonwalk around the stage? Stand on the tips of both toes? Maybe a pelvic thrust?

For some strange reason, Michael just stood there as if he was frozen in time. The instruments kept playing as the drum beat to

"Billy Jean" got louder, and *then it happened*!

Michael Jackson suddenly hunched over, grimacing in pain. No one in the audience knew what to think. All of the entertainers knew how to be in front of a camera, completely engrossed in their respective characters as the camera rolled, but this seemed different.

The icon of iconic figures was standing before them, as real as real could be, seemingly in horrible pain.

Actor Don Cheadle held up his sign, "E. D., this is going too far, even for you."

While the whole room was in chaos, the camera panned back to E. D., showing no emotion whatsoever. Contrarily, Evelyn looked confused while spanning and searching for the security of her husband's eyes.

Just then, megastar Alicia Keys walked up to within a few feet of her childhood idol to see if he was okay.

"Get away!" he said. Alicia and everyone in the room screamed in horror. There he was, the king of pop, with yellow ghoulish eyes, having suddenly grown fangs, claws, and whiskers. It was then that the camera went quickly to E. D. with one of the biggest smiles ever.

Alicia and her friends just realized that they had been part of a great prank while witnessing one of the greatest music videos of all time. It originally aired on December 2, 1983, and since that time, it has had more than 149 million views on YouTube. Evelyn had no idea that Michael would be part of her next question.

As the AI (artificial intelligence) version of Michael Jackson stood frozen again, having this fixed horrifying expression on his face, E. D. asked Evelyn her final question of the round. "Evelyn, what is the name of Michael Jackson's song that included him looking like this insurmountable monster?"

Now at ease, Evelyn, well aware this new and improved *Jeopardy!* show was all about entertainment, delayed giving her answer while rising from her chair as she confidently strutted a few steps before she yelled confidently, "What is… 'Thriller!'"

"That's correct! Congratulations, Evelyn, you've just won $5,000."

E. D. looked at Evelyn and added, "The best part of recording the show is that we are able to take a real break to give everyone a chance to regroup. Your total thus far is $17,500. We will start again in 15 minutes."

Chapter 2: Intermission

During the short intermission, one of the actresses walked up to Evelyn to say hello. "Hi, my name is Amanda." Evelyn shook Amanda's hand, trying to remember where she had seen her before.

"Amanda," Evelyn asked, "are you part of the show? Were you sitting in the audience, or are you working backstage? And why is it that you're the first entertainer to actually speak? I get the whole idea of holding up the questions and answers, but it's odd that no one actually has talked to me except for you."

"Evelyn, I don't have much time, and I can't explain it right now, but you need to take a look into the ears of the stars who are holding up the signs." Suddenly, Amanda caught eyes with E. D. He gave her a look that said, "Not another word."

Evelyn noticed the exchange between E. D. and Amanda and quickly changed course.

"I remember now; I saw you on a late-night talk show one night back in 2016. I only caught the last minute of your conversation with Stephen Colbert."

Amanda cringed, recalling what happened that night. Many times after that show aired, she found herself explaining to others what people called a meltdown.

Amanda looked at Evelyn and said, "When Stephen started pressing me about the idea of me having a midlife crisis, something inside of me just burst, and the three words that I had locked away for so many years came gushing out. After I said them, the entire conversation grew like a swelling wave in the ocean. When it crashed, I felt even worse because I still didn't have an answer to the horrible dilemma that follows me around each and every day of my life. Evelyn, I can't stop thinking about it."

Evelyn felt a deep compassion for Amanda as she put her arm around her and asked, "What did you say that night?" Amanda buried her head in Evelyn's side just about the same time E. D. walked over to them and said, "Ladies, it's time to start again."

Double Jeopardy

"Welcome back, everyone. I'm your host, E. D. Raines, and we're back with Evelyn Dawson, who has amassed $17,500 in round one. Are you ready to play Double Jeopardy?"

Though disturbed over the strange happenings, Evelyn got it together, knowing that she had to do a little acting of her own. "Absolutely, E. D.!"

"Is everyone in the audience ready? How about you, Tom Hanks?" Tom gave E. D. that shy, wry smile and a thumbs-up toward E. D. and Evelyn. And with that, Tom stood up to speak but was unable to do so. He reached down for the card that had the question and held it up for Evelyn to read. It read, "Evelyn, here is your first Double Jeopardy question. You will have 30 seconds to give me as many 'one-word' movie titles associated with the actors' names that I hold up. Please put 30 seconds on the clock."

Tom held up, "Mel Gibson!"

Evelyn answered, "*Braveheart!*"

"Joaquin Phoenix"

"*Batman* and *Gladiator!*"

When Tom held up "Julia Roberts," Evelyn drew a blank.

Then Tom held up "Meryl Streep," and Evelyn drew another blank.

Tom simply couldn't resist the challenge, knowing that Evelyn had just passed on the last two names.

Tom's next sign said, "Me!"

With only 10 seconds remaining, Evelyn answered, "*Big, Castaway, Sully, Philadelphia,* and *Splash*!"

The buzzer sounded off!

"Fantastic Job, Evelyn," said E. D. "Each correct answer was worth $2,000. You got eight correct answers, worth another $16,000. You have almost doubled what you had at the break, with a total of $33,500. Here's question 2: famous last words. Evelyn, I'm going to read some famous people's last words, but leaving out one word. Please fill in the blank with the correct one. I'd like to ask legendary shortstop Derek Jeter to stand up and reveal the next question."

Evelyn looked into Derek's ear and saw that he was wearing only one earpiece. Derek held up his card, which read, "Hi, Evelyn. As you might expect, this is going to be a Yankee question. The late Joe DiMaggio said, 'I finally get to see again!' Who or what does Mr. DiMaggio finally get to see?"

Evelyn, thinking to herself, thought about the song by Simon and Garfunkel that had a small mention of Joe DiMaggio.

Evelyn looked at E. D. and said, "I honestly don't know the answer, but because he was such a great player while alive, I'm going to say, 'What is…baseball'? I think that Joe DiMaggio would want to see a baseball knowing he can play the game he loved, forever in heaven."

"No, I'm sorry, Evelyn, the right answer is Marilyn. Joe was referring to seeing Marilyn Monroe again. That's going to cost you $2,000, dropping your total, but still a comfortable $31,500.

LeBron, will you please stand up and ask Evelyn question three?"

E. D. turned to Evelyn, saying, "This one is for $3,000."

LeBron stood up and smiled at Evelyn, holding up his card that read, "You're doing great. You can beat him."

His card read, "One of the most elite ball handlers in the NBA was a man with a great nickname, Pistol Pete Maravich. Sadly, after playing in a pick-up basketball game at the age of forty, he had a heart attack. Can you tell us Pete's last words as he lay there dying?"

Before Evelyn could answer, LeBron took a sneak peek at the answer on the back of his card and then suddenly blurted out, "Is that right?"

E. D. whispered into LeBron's earpiece, "Really, LeBron? Not another word."

Evelyn thought she might have the right answer until hearing LeBron speak up like that. *Obviously*, she thought to herself, *the answer may not be what I imagined*, but she took her guess.

"What is: 'I feel nauseous'?"

"I'm so sorry, Evelyn; the right answer was 'Great'!"

"Wow," said Evelyn, "I don't think those would be my last words."

LeBron wanted to speak. He wanted to apologize to Evelyn for confusing her, but he knew he had better not. Instead, he got out a black marker and wrote this on another card. "E. D., please don't take away $3,000 from her. I'll take the hit."

"Folks," said E. D. "This is why we have created this new version of *Jeopardy!* Thanks, LeBron!"

E. D. looked into the crowd of entertainers and caught the eyes of Tim Tebow. They looked at each other for a few seconds until (as rehearsed) he stood up and pointed back at E. D., who yelled out, "Daily Double Time!"

Calmly, E. D. sat back down and looked straight at Evelyn while he addressed Tim, saying, "Okay, Tim, we can all see that the card you're holding up isn't a card at all; it's a Bible. We all know you to be a man of faith."

Turning toward Evelyn, Tim noticed that she looked a little uncomfortable, so he said, "Evelyn, you're going to do just fine. I prayed for whoever was going to be the contestant to be relaxed and ready to recall whatever question I was asked to give. Are you ready?" Evelyn nodded as she put her hands together as if she was praying. And then it hit her: Tim actually spoke words!

"Wait," E. D. said, "I almost forgot, Evelyn, how much would you like to risk on this question?"

Now confident, Evelyn said, "$10,000!"

"Okay, Tim, ask the question!"

Tim opened the Bible to the beginning, the book of Genesis. He smiled as he first read it silently to himself. Looking at Evelyn, he asked, "What are the first five words in the Bible!" Evelyn had the biggest grin on her face as she caught eyes with Tim. She knew this answer. She had been taught all her life to answer such a question. Thinking about 10,000 more dollars and how that would really help with her children's education, she slowly said, "In the beginning, man existed!"

Tim was stunned, preparing to respond. Evelyn saw her husband, Jeff, standing off stage with his right fist raised in the air, ready to celebrate. E. D. whispered into Tim's ear and said, "It's my turn now!"

"Evelyn Dawson, *you just won $10,000!*"

The audience of stars went crazy. Most everyone was cheering for Evelyn. Evelyn looked over at Jeff and whispered the words, "I love you," and just as fast, "Where are the girls?"

Jeff replied, "They're fine."

E. D. stood up, motioning with his hands for the crowd to settle down. Evelyn and E. D. sat down once again to catch their collective breaths. E. D. asked, "How does all this feel, Evelyn?"

"E. D., today is one of the greatest days of my life. Thank you for this opportunity."

"Before we get to Final Jeopardy," said E. D. "I'm going to show you two words that will complete the Double Jeopardy round: *your life*! Evelyn, from your original application, we took all the information you supplied us with and used our new *Jeopardy!* computer algorithm process to best describe who you are through two of the songs you were most affected by. There isn't a question in this round; no money to win or lose, just a way of telling the entertainers and those at home watching just who you are at the core."

Evelyn looked at E. D. with a different sense of excitement. She wondered what the computer figured out about her. She knew that in her heart, family was the most important aspect of her life, and she had conveyed that in her application. Evelyn had no idea of which entertainer would stand up next, but whoever it was, she would be excited.

There would be no introduction from E. D. Within the first two notes, Evelyn's heart dropped, and her eyes filled with tears when she heard the piano and the first word, "Memories," as legendary singer Barbara Streisand slowly stood up.

E. D. wanted the right effect for this segment of the show. After all, *Jeopardy!* was still all about entertainment. With a recording of Barbara softly singing the words in the background, Barbara came up to the stage to embrace Evelyn through the song she had heard over 5,000 times in her lifetime.

Barbara asked Evelyn to explain what the song "The Way We Were" meant to her. Evelyn drifted back into her teen years, recalling a song that made her cry every time. "Barbara, my memories continue to sit in the corners of my mind. They are, indeed, misty and watercolored, but not just about the start and finish of every fractured couple who were once in love with one another; it's mostly about the way we really were as people. Barbara, every time I hear the words 'scattered pictures' come from your mouth, I think of all the wonderful people I've come to know and love in my life. Yes, the smiles we have to leave behind as we lose contact with high-school or college friends are difficult, but I love holding onto those thoughts."

"Barbara," Evelyn continued, "you are so right. There was a time in my life when things were much simpler. And yes, time has indeed written every line. But when I think to myself, *If I had the chance to do life all over again, would I?* You bet I would."

Barbara quietly sang the song that Evelyn had locked away for so long. She stood there having a real connection to her favorite female singer of all time, Barbara Streisand. As Barbara sang the last note of "The Way We Were," Barbara and Evelyn embraced each other. And then, just like that, Barbara slowly turned and walked out of the theater.

By chance, one of *Jeopardy!*'s cameras caught E. D. with his head down, wiping away the tears from his eyes. Evelyn's eyes were looking offstage for her husband, Jeff, but he wasn't anywhere to be found.

E. D., having regained his composure, looked at Evelyn with a smile, "Now that hit my heart!"

Evelyn responded with, "A moment I'll never forget. I can't even imagine what's next."

"Do you want to see?" asked E. D.

The lights went down low to where you could barely see the person in front of you. Then, a spotlight hit the one empty chair perfectly positioned in the back of the room.

Up on the monitor popped the man who made the ladies swoon long before the Beatles came on the scene. The singer-actor who typically had a cigarette in one hand and a martini in the other, the one and only Frank Sinatra!

Evelyn got goosebumps just hearing his name. She grew up in the house of her late parents, who had played many of Frank Sinatra's songs to her and her siblings while growing up. Hoping to hear "New York, New York," having grown up there, she was a little shocked when she heard a different song begin to play. It was Sinatra's "My Way."

E. D. looked Evelyn in the eye and said, "As we get to the end of the show, not only did our *Jeopardy!* computer system spit this song out as one of the two songs to best describe you, but our singers, actors, and athletes love this song so much as well that they want to participate in it with you. We've chosen a portion of the song to convey what we know about you."

E. D. whispered to everyone, "Make sure we get this right. When I call your name, hold that sign up high!"

When E. D. yelled, "Now!" one by one, the actors stood up one at a time, holding up their respective signs for Evelyn to see.

Adele's sign said, "Evelyn, we have something in common."

Jennifer Lopez's sign said, "Evelyn, you're like me too."

Robert Downey Jr.'s sign said, "Evelyn, we all do it a certain way."

A couple of older fan favorites chimed in, too.

Robert De Niro's sign said, "Life is about doing it this way."

Al Pacino's sign said, "Evelyn, I agree. You have to look out for number one."

Suddenly, Tom Brady, Lebron, Madonna, The Rock (Dwayne Johnson), Adam Sandler, Taylor Swift, Beyonce, Jennifer Aniston, and Jimmy Fallon all stood up, one fist in the air and yelled,

"Evelyn, *we did it our way*! Just like Frank Sinatra said."

Before Evelyn had a chance to process what she had just seen, E. D. beamed with joy, saying, "Evelyn, your life has been so successful. You've lived as a banker, making and spending money. You're happily married and a mother of two. You've played sports, traveled around the world, and loved and heard all of the best music of the past seventy years. Frank stood for doing it his way, the same way as all these stars before you. It takes hard work to get where you are in life. The stars have something to say to you: 'Evelyn, we're going to miss you when your game is over.'"

"I'll miss you too," said Evelyn.

"Evelyn, in all of the emotions of the moment, I almost forgot that we have a game to finish," said E. D. "But this is what I love best about the show."

Chapter 3: Final Jeopardy

"You have $41,500 up to this point. Do you remember what I told you at the beginning of the show? You have to be in the black to win. So be careful what you wager."

"The Final Jeopardy category is: 'Who Am I?'"

Here's the question, "Evelyn, what do my initials, E. D., stand for?"

E. D. saw the incredulous look on Evelyn's face. She had never anticipated a question like this. She knew that E. D. had to be up to something, some kind of trick.

Evelyn went back in her mind to the introduction of the show, trying to figure it out. Part of the new and improved version of the *Jeopardy!* game was what they called second chances, or in ordinary terms, helpful hints. E. D., sensing that Evelyn might need some assistance, said, "Evelyn, would you like to use your one helpful hint? If you do, it will cost you."

Evelyn gave an exasperated look and said to herself, "Really? I have to pay for the hint?"

"Yes, but it only costs two dollars."

Evelyn and everyone watching chuckled. "Yes, I think I'll risk it."

"Don Maclean, please stand up!"

"I love this song!" said Evelyn.

E. D. looked at her and said, "He hasn't started singing yet!"

"I know," said Evelyn, "but there's only one song of his that everyone knows."

"Ouch!" said Don, with a wry smile. "Yes, Evelyn, although I wrote other songs, this is the one most people have listened to, whether it was sitting in their cars or hanging out with friends in a bar. But you are right! 'American Pie' is the song, but that's not your helpful hint; this is, Evelyn, 'This will be the day that you die!'"

Everyone let out a collective gasp. Evelyn's mouth fell open, appearing to be in shock when Evelyn suddenly burst out laughing.

"That's funny. I have sung your song so many times, and now, the hint I get on one of the most prestigious shows has my name personally being included in your song? E. D., that was incredibly clever," said Evelyn.

E. D. looked over at Evelyn and said, "I wasn't being clever, Evelyn. Don Maclean said it right. Your hint is, *'This will be the day that you die'*! So I'll ask you again, can you tell me what my initials, E. D., stand for?"

Okay, Evelyn thought to herself. *Let me just get this question right, collect my money, wave to the stars, find my family, and leave so I can go home.*

She remembered their introduction. Composing herself and focusing on the hint, trying to figure out what in the world was going on, she went back over the game one more time. There certainly was a theme to it all, but as she sat on national television, in front of her favorite entertainers, with all of her friends watching from home, the last thing she wanted was to be the laughingstock of the world.

Slowly, Evelyn looked at E. D. and said, "Before I answer the question, I want to say something. In my heart of hearts, I don't think you're asking for a regular name; I think your initials are the theme of the show; am I right?"

E. D. stared at Evelyn in silence but wouldn't answer.

"Okay, I guess that means no," Evelyn said while looking out into the audience. After taking another 10 seconds or so, she was ready to answer. "My answer is Evelyn's Dream!"

Before E. D. could respond, Evelyn continued, "Wow, this has been the wildest dream I've ever had. When I wake up, I'm going to let Jeff and the girls really have it for hiding in most of it."

"Evelyn," E. D. said with great conviction, "your answer of 'Evelyn's Dream' is incorrect! The correct answer is Evelyn's Death!"

Evelyn sat there speechless as E. D. explained, "The show began with a thud. It was when you fell to the ground in the kitchen of your home while watching your favorite show, *Jeopardy!* You had a heart attack, Evelyn.

"Here is where I come in. My name is Death! And whoever it is that's dying, that becomes my first initial. 'Evelyn's Death' is my name today, and your death is my priority. By the way, your heart has stopped beating for over three minutes now. The reason you couldn't find your children was your fear of one day never seeing them again. Did you notice the two earpieces in all of the entertainers' ears? Have you figured out why they wouldn't or why they couldn't talk out loud during the game? You see, they listen to me. I'm in charge. That woman, Amanda, the one you talked to during intermission, tried to tell you, but I stopped her before she could share it with you. Yes, you have been kept in the dark about what's really going on around you all of your life until now. Right now, you're in an ambulance on the way to the hospital, but it's going to be too late. Your husband, Jeff, and your girls are driving behind you; that's why you couldn't find them in your game. You don't believe me, do you? Do you remember me putting a blanket on you early in the game?"

"Yes," said Evelyn.

"Well, that was because your circulation system was shutting down due to the blood clot that's in one of your main arteries."

Evelyn was in a full-on panic. She looked out into the audience of megastars, trying to understand why they were there in the first place.

"I know," said E. D., turning to Evelyn. "You can't fully grasp the gravity of the situation. Evelyn, you are dying! All of the actors and entertainers that you see have contributed to all of the stored-up images, songs, sayings, and faces during your lifespan. The lyrics to so many songs that you and many people have listened to have caused internal stress that many are not even aware of. The words to the songs 'Piano Man' and 'Eleanor Rigby' have been suffocating the inner person of who you really are. Think about it, Evelyn: the song 'Eleanor Rigby' starts out strangely enough with us listening to it, causing us to picture and wonder why there are so many lonely people around the world. And where is the origin? How many times have you listened to the song 'Piano Man' and how Billy Joel described the feeling of those sitting in the bar? A lonely place with one small solace. At least everyone is sharing their drink and loneliness together."

E.D. looked at Evelyn and asked her a question, "Do you really think everyone in the world who is highly successful, rich, and famous, like these people, is happy deep down on the inside?"

Evelyn stood there with a blank stare until he said, "You stored away the word 'Shallow' as you listened to Lady Gaga and Bradley Cooper sing their song into your soul. Yes, it's true from the words that you've heard over and over again; Evelyn, you've been trying to 'fill that void' with movies, games, and songs that, at best, have only told you how many people feel, but never go far enough to solve the main problem, the need that fills all emptiness!"

Evelyn quickly interrupted, still not fully grasping the situation. "Okay, fine. Let's say I believe you that I'm dying. If I really am in an ambulance right now with the paramedics trying to revive my dying body, then how and why are we talking?"

    E. D. grinned and said, "You still don't get it, do you? Take a look at the screen just in front of you."

    There she was, Amanda, the woman she spoke to at intermission. "Evelyn," said E. D. "Do you remember Amanda trying to tell you about what she said on the Colbert show?" Evelyn nodded. "Well, now I'm ready to show you."

***

    The date was February 18, 2016. Stephen said, "You have a new HBO hit called *Togetherness* about a woman who is dealing with a midlife crisis. You don't look like a woman in crisis."

    Amanda replied, "Well, it's ongoing." She squirmed in her seat.

    Stephen said, "What's your crisis? What do you worry about?"

    Amanda replied, "I fear death!"

    After Stephen reminded her that she was on a late-night comedy show and to keep it light, Amanda hadn't gotten it all out of her hiding spot. She tried a more lighthearted approach and said to Stephen, "I'm Jewish, and you're Catholic, so we are the same, right?"

    Stephen, never to miss an opportunity for a laugh, said, "Catholics are the Jews of Christianity."

    Stephen, seeing that Amanda was not amused, said, "Hey, maybe you'll go to heaven."

    Amanda, crying out to the world, said, "I need to know what to believe in. I don't want to be a bag of dust."

***

As the episode faded out in front of them both, E. D. said to Evelyn, "Amanda was in your personal game because deep down inside, the two of you and billions more live your lives as if they're never going to end. All of you are petrified of me, kidding about me in public but never wanting to deal with me."

Evelyn, with a wounded look, asked, "Am I really dying right now?"

Before E. D. could answer, Evelyn, with one last bit of determination and logic, mustered up the strength to say, "None of this makes any sense unless you can explain the part of me playing this game for money and whether or not I finished the game in the black; and in case you forgot, I did finish in the black."

E. D., with a sarcastic tone, said, "Did you really, Evelyn? You had $41,500 before Final Jeopardy, correct?"

Evelyn nodded.

"Well," said E. D. "I know what you wagered."

Evelyn answered, "How could you? I never showed it to you or the audience; there, see! I only wagered $41,499, so I still finished $1 in the black."

"Evelyn, if you had finished in the black, it meant you would have been revived in the ambulance and been able to see me at a later date down the road, but you did lose the game, Evelyn, because you forgot about the cost of the last helpful hint. Do you remember? It cost $2." Amanda's head dropped as she remembered. "Therefore," said E. D., showing absolutely no remorse for tricking Evelyn, "you will die and die in the red, or as I tell many, you will die in debt!"

Evelyn screamed, "In debt to what?"

Fear gripped every part of Evelyn's body when suddenly a great and unexpected struggle ensued between some of the entertainers and E. D.

The Battle Begins

Paul Simon and Art Garfunkel stood up and removed their earpieces, looked at Evelyn with sadness in their eyes, and said, "Evelyn, it is our sincere hope that you will listen to us now the way you did when you heard us on the radio. Many of our songs were spiritual in nature. Think Evelyn think. Our song 'The Sound of Silence' talked about a friend named darkness. We wrote about words of prophets that were written on the walls down at the subway station. Evelyn, there have been so many clues for your soul to grab onto, including one of our little-known songs called 'Old Friends.' It was a slow song that was intended to remind our listeners that at a moment's notice, a person is suddenly seventy years old, and what's left are memories and a very real fear of death. Evelyn Dawson, we only have one question to ask you, 'Do you know Jesus?'"

Evelyn was overcome with emotion, literally sobbing right in front of E. D., who only had one thing to say, "Too late, boys. She's mine."

E. D. whispered into the ear of Gary Sinise, also known as Lieutenant Dan, in the blockbuster movie *Forrest Gump*, "Tell Evelyn what you said to Tom Hanks when you were depressed, sitting in your wheelchair with long, scraggly hair, staring at the television set, watching people celebrate New Year's."

Gary looked at Evelyn and said, "The Hollywood writers gave me a script which told me to ask Tom if he had 'found Jesus yet.'"

E. D. chimed in and said, "I'll take it from here, Gary, thanks. Evelyn, you saw this movie so many times and heard what Forrest Gump said yet did nothing about it. Do you remember now? Let me refresh your memory. Forrest, in his childlike way, admitted that he had no idea that he was supposed to be looking for Jesus. Evelyn, you didn't either because as you got older, you shut out anyone who wanted to talk to you concerning what happens after we die while at the same time playing a big game of hide and seek with me."

Evelyn looked around the room one more time for her family, still refusing to believe that she had died.

E. D., seeing an opportunity to make Evelyn feel even worse, sarcastically said, "Even I know what the first five words of the Bible say."

"What? Now, wait just a minute," said Evelyn. "I got that question right. You told me so, remember? I said, 'In the beginning, man existed,' and you gave me the money."

"Evelyn, I lied! Your answer was wrong! Tim, tell Evelyn the right answer."

Tim, with tears of compassion, looked at Evelyn and said, "In the beginning, God created."

Evelyn felt the sting of betrayal like never before, having been lied to by E. D. But just as fast, she felt the shame of living all of her life not knowing what the Bible says. She also wondered to herself why Tim didn't say anything when she actually got the answer wrong.

"Why? Because Tim Tebow isn't dying right now, you are, and I simply used all of your memories, including the moments you watched Tim Tebow play football or talk about his faith against you. He meant them for good, but I twisted them to confuse you."

Evelyn felt paralyzed with fear yet had the strength to say, "So what happens when other people die? What's your name, then?"

"Sometimes I'm called A. D. for people like Adele or Alicia Keys. Sometimes, I'm L. D., after LeBron. All I do is change my initials and play the same Final Jeopardy game with everyone who has died or is dying. Evelyn, do you know what my favorite initials are? T. D."

"Is that why you brought Tom Hanks, Tiger Woods, and Tom

Brady into my game?" asked Evelyn.

"I didn't bring them in, you did. These are the people that you kept in your mind for all these years. But since you did bring them up, I can tell you that they will meet me one day, and I will wear their initials, and they will most certainly play their final games, not with any golf ball, football, or movie about themselves, but with me personally. Evelyn? Have you figured out who I really am yet? I'm T. D., *the devil*! I'm the one responsible for your death and your lifelong fear of death. Most people don't think I really exist. Others make light of me. Do you remember your favorite college basketball team? It's the Duke Blue Devils. Do you see how easy it is? Place my name onto a sports team, and everyone cheers. My name is loved on the East Coast, too, with the New Jersey Devils hockey team. I know you remember the late comedian of the '70s, Flip Wilson. His tagline was, 'The devil made me do it.' The human race makes a joke out of me while the Bible tells all about me, and what's shocking about it all is what the Bible says about all of us who are against the name of Jesus Christ, 'Even the demons believe and shudder.' We know He's real, but we help men and women curse His name during basketball games or when yelling at someone in anger. It's almost too easy! And why? Because most men don't believe in Him or me."

T. D. had this combination look of hate and satisfaction as he glanced into Evelyn's eyes.

Evelyn cried out, "Oh, God, please save me!"

"Too late! You had your chances again and again. You did it your way! Like Frank Sinatra sang, which is really my way! Sally Fields, stand up and tell Evelyn the truth. When you played Momma to your son Forrest, and he asked you why you were dying, what script did Hollywood give you?"

Sally stood up, ready to answer, when E. D. cut her off, saying, "Hollywood told you a lie! It's much more than 'it's something we're all destined to do.'"

The devil looked at Evelyn and Sally, saying, "I don't see any harm in telling you both now. Everyone dies because they have sinned against God. Tell her the other truth, Sally."

Sally said, "Life isn't like a box of chocolates, not knowing what we get! We get our choices."

The devil looked Sally straight in the eyes and said, "Thank you, Sally, now disappear!" Sally slowly vanished right before Evelyn's eyes.

"What just happened to Sally?" screamed Evelyn.

"Nothing yet, she's still living. She still has time. But if she dies believing that death is just a part of life, believing the Hollywood script instead of the Bible, then at her death, my initials will be S. D."

Evelyn responded with, "Sally's death?"

"No, Evelyn, much worse…the Second Death!

"This death will be worse than physical death, and much to my hate and disgust, the writer of this book will be trying to convince as many readers as possible to pick up the Bible and find out how not to have this death happen. But I am very confident because I know that many people will close their ears to the truth and believe me and my lies."

Evelyn began to cry, "I was a good person! I never killed anyone."

The devil whispered into the ear of Don Maclean to tell Evelyn another truth.

"Evelyn, did you ever listen to the song from the Charlie Daniels Band, 'The Devil Went Down to Georgia'?"

"Yes, of course, everyone did!" said Evelyn.

"Did you believe it?" asked Don. "Please be honest?"

"No, not really," said Evelyn.

"Well, that's probably why you didn't believe the other words in my song. People have always focused on the one line about the day of one's death, usually while at some Friday night party holding up a beer. Everybody sings that line like death is some type of joy or nothing to worry about. But the truth is that no one knows that what they are actually doing is stuffing it all away into some deep, dark 'hiding spot.' At the same time, Evelyn, my song mentioned a book of love where I asked the listener if they had faith in God above. Evelyn, do you remember now?" Don could see her face beginning to smile.

"What about the next line?" Don asked.

Evelyn mouthed the words quietly to herself when it suddenly hit her. She jumped up with great excitement, saying, "I don't remember the line exactly, but I know it had to do with the Bible."

Don then said, "I am glad you are starting to remember Evelyn. It makes all the difference in the end." Don had one more reminder he wanted to share with Evelyn. "In my song, I even made a point of asking the world if music could save their mortal souls. The answer is yes if music leads a person to pick up a Bible and read about the only one who can save us from our sins. Now, do you remember?"

"Yes, yes, thank you, Don, I do remember. Though my parents didn't spend much time teaching me, I once knew that the Bible is God's book of truth that tells man where they came from and who God is. I really see that now!"

T. D. had a look of great satisfaction when he said to Evelyn, "It's too late for you, Evelyn! That's one of the consequences of dying before finding out the truth. And it was your choice to ignore it for all of your life."

Simon and Garfunkel stood up together and shouted, "Evelyn, don't ever forget who loves you the most. It's Jesus who died for your sins."

"Whoa, boys! Enough!" T. D. said.

"Sorry, E. D. We removed your earpieces a long time ago," they said. "We don't listen to you anymore."

"Guys, she's dead!"

Paul Simon caught eyes with James Taylor, as he immediately stood up, not wearing an earpiece either. A sense of comfort came over her as T. D. stood there motionless.

"Evelyn, the reason I'm here is because you have stored away one of my songs that can help you right now. It is called 'Fire and Rain.' Do you remember it?"

"Yes!" Evelyn said with excitement.

"In it, I asked for God to look down upon me," said James. "Specifically, didn't you ask Jesus to?" Evelyn asked.

"That's right, Evelyn, I asked Jesus to help me make a stand! Evelyn, it's the stand that goes against this lying and hateful angel who wouldn't serve God because he wanted to be God and the one who tries to pounce on every believer by twisting the truth to make us doubt the love of God, causing us to do it our own way. People will find this out later in the book, much to the hate of T. D., but the joy of finding out the truth, I'm about to tell you, is the most priceless piece of wisdom anyone can ever know. It's what you, Amanda, and everyone in the world need to hear. Jesus Christ is the only one who can take away the fear of death. Evelyn, this is why, in my song, you can almost hear my pain as I implore Jesus to help me, knowing that He's the only way."

Suddenly, like a bolt of lightning, Oprah Winfrey stood up and yelled out, "Jesus can't be the only way to heaven!"

T. D. stood there with a smile on his face, saying, "Take a look in her ears, Evelyn; my earpieces are in both of them. She believes in God; in fact, she has said that she's a Christian but refuses to believe what Jesus says about Himself."

"I am the way, and the truth, and the life. No one comes to the Father except through me" (John 14:6).

"I put those ideas into Oprah's mind through the years. I convince many people to believe in Jesus as the Christ, but not that He's the only way or the only door to heaven. Sure, I'll lose a few, but I'll gain so many more who want to get to heaven through a different door. This is one of my favorite lies of all."

Without any warning, Hall of Fame Quarterback Kurt Warner stood up.

"Evelyn, I know that you and your husband, Jeff, love sports. Do you remember the Superbowl that my team, the St. Louis Rams, won when we beat the Tennessee Titans?"

"Absolutely," said Evelyn.

"Sit down, Kurt!" screamed T. D.

"I can't hear you, T. D. Evelyn, my words that day for people to hear were, 'Thank You, Jesus!' The devil knows this; don't be fooled. He also knows that Jesus continues to be preached and followed because the human soul desires one thing…to live, Evelyn! Jesus is the only one who died for the world, and He proved it by being resurrected from the dead. He is alive, Evelyn! And He offers eternal life to a world of sinners!"

T. D. furiously looked away from Kurt and glared back at Evelyn, trying to shame her by saying, "You may know about Jesus, but you don't know Jesus like Kurt Warner does."

Without hesitation, T. D. shouted, "*Meet Joe Black*!" Suddenly, Brad Pitt stood up.

"Evelyn, Brad played me, Death! Not exactly like the real thing here today, but extremely effective."

"Why in the world would he or anyone want to play the part of Death?" Evelyn asked.

"Because it's powerful! You get to have so much authority. And I'm sure it pays well in Hollywood. Just ask Al Pacino when he played me in the movie *The Devil's Advocate*. Don't you get it, Evelyn? There's a movie named after me, songs after me, scripts that are for me and against God, and many people hear it, stuff it away, but never connect the spiritual dots. Then they die, and it's too late. Just like you. Evelyn, do you remember ever having chest pains before?"

"Yes, a few times," Evelyn answered.

"Well, that's what happened in the movie *Meet Joe Black*. Sir Anthony Hopkins plays a rich man named Bill, who suddenly has chest pains and begins thinking about his own mortality, just like you. When Brad played me, he did exactly what I really do in people's lives: question their own mortality. But it's much more than that, Evelyn; it's when characters like Bill, who are rich and full of life, come to grips with the fact that all of this will end: the money, the fame, and most importantly, time. People want time. They love time. But I have come to take that time away. Do you want to know what people fear the most about death? It's not knowing what's next and yet knowing that something is very wrong! Most never figure it out! So, they stuff the question away or just laugh it off. In fact, there's a poll that says that man's greatest fear is public speaking—another lie. Make no mistake, the fear of me is man's greatest fear; you could even say that death scares them to death!"

There was a pause until T. D. said, "Evelyn, I have something to tell you."

"Well, you rebellious and disparaging spirit," said Evelyn, "I have something to tell you, too. You can't hurt me anymore. I believe Kurt Warner, James Taylor, and Simon and Garfunkel. I truly believe in Jesus Christ."

"Evelyn, I was just going to say that they just pronounced you dead in the hospital. There was a faint hope of you being revived. The paramedics got you to the hospital after shocking your heart three times, but your heart attack was simply too severe. You died at exactly 3 p.m. There will be no more birthdays, anniversaries, or joyful holidays. Your obituary will read, 'Evelyn leaves behind a loving husband, Jeff, two beautiful children, Adeline and Victoria, along with a host full of memories concerning her favorite actors, athletes, movies, and songs.' And it will say nothing about you seeking the truth or believing in Jesus, and you won't be able to tell the truth about me. The only thing you can do is live for eternity in fear, calling out to God without Him hearing you. And much to my joy, this will be revealed later in this book. Oh yes, many of your family members will be there at your funeral, along with your friends at the bank and a few others who still remember you from high school. The preacher, or whoever speaks about your life, will most certainly preach you into heaven for being a good person. He will quote a few scriptures to make everyone feel better about not seeing you again. In fact, he will tell everyone that you are looking down at them from above. Don't you find it strange, Evelyn, that no one ever says, 'He or she is looking up from down below?' That would be too much for the human heart to bear, wouldn't it? Evelyn, you and I are going to be condemned, or as the Bible says...*lost*. There are a few who get away from going where we're headed because they found out that I was a liar and saw the truth about how to be *saved*...but you won't be one of them."

    Evelyn screamed at the top of her lungs as T. D. took her by the hand to escort her to his home.

    Out of nowhere, a young girl in a white dress stood up and walked toward Evelyn. She reached for her hand. The devil held firm to Evelyn's left hand while this mystery girl softly grabbed her right.

    T. D. looked at the young girl and said, "I see you're wearing the other kind of earpiece, the one with the initials T. S., 'the

Savior.' And I can see from the way you're dressed that you follow Jesus, but there's nothing you can do to change this outcome, young lady. This woman has died, and she's going to be with me for all eternity."

"Then I guess you were the one not listening," said the young lady. "Because if you had, then you would have heard me and my sister, Adeline, praying to God through Jesus for our mother. Here's the answer to our prayer."

The faint sound of a piano began to play within earshot of T. D. He recognized the song right from the start, letting out a soothing "Ahhhhh," after which he said, "Now this is one of my all-time favorite songs."

With a serious look into the eyes of T. D., the young lady spoke, "I guess you haven't quite understood my prayer to God, D. D."

In disgust, T. D.'s head snapped back as he sniped at the young lady, "What did you call me?"

With incredible courage, the young woman said, "After you hear my new words to your song, it will be the end of you, or Death's Death, instead of my mother's."

"I don't know what you are up to," said T. D., "but the song 'Imagine' is one of my finest works ever. Getting John Lennon to continually plant doubts in the minds of all people around the globe as to whether there really is a heaven or not was and always will be so delightfully satisfying. The only thing better than that was convincing John and many other religious groups in the world today that there is no hell below us."

Suddenly, it hit T. D. right where it hurt. "Young lady, maybe I didn't hear you correctly, but did you say that the words have been changed?" T. D. continued, "Do you really think people are going to accept your words over John Lennon's?"

Without hesitation, the young lady decided to describe her version by singing the song herself while she looked straight into the soul of T. D.

T. D. screamed in pain as he went down to the ground on one knee. "How dare you say that the world should imagine that there's a heaven!" With every line, T. D. felt more and more pain, yet with the resolve of only hate in his heart, he fought back. "I convinced John Lennon and billions of people that they should live for today, yet you come here with your song of faith, telling everyone that they can live for eternity in a wonderful place? You are literally killing me. I have tricked the majority of souls into believing, as John Lennon said, that the world is a better place without religion. Yet, today, you are singing words to me that suggest to people that they should imagine a place where there is no depression, crying, pain, or hunger?"

The young lady, feeling the strength and grace of God in her heart, raised her voice and spoke a truth that jolted T. D., "You are the ultimate lying deceiver, just like it says in the Bible. You are the father of lies. My next line will put you back where you belong and out of my mother's life. My favorite line to *Imagine*'s new song is, 'Imagine a place where no one is sinning! And imagine living in a place of peace for all eternity in heaven with God.'" And with the final blow, the young lady said, "You may say that I am a Christian, T. D., but I am not the only one. One day, we will all praise God on bended knees because we don't have to imagine that there's a Savior. We already know for sure that there is. He is Jesus Christ, the Savior of the world, who came to die and take us to the Father, who absolutely, 100 percent lives above the sky."

With one last gasp of air, T. D. whispered into the young lady's ear as he began loosening his grip on Evelyn, "How could you do this to me? Those lyrics of mine through John Lennon made him so much money and brought him great fame and allowed me to watch the doubts of people's souls grow farther away from the truth."

Suddenly, without any warning, a song from the 1970s began to play. It was a song by the group "Kansas." T. D.'s face went limp, knowing what he was about to hear. And with that, the young lady whispered into the earpiece of T. D., "Do you remember the song? It was called 'Dust in the Wind,' and that's what you are."

Suddenly, a beep was heard, like that of a truck backing up. Then another beep, and another until T. D. knew. Evelyn's heart started again.

Evelyn watched T. D. disappear like sand falling through someone's fingers. He was dead to her.

In the Hospital

The doctors and nurses rushed into Evelyn's room, where she had been pronounced dead.

They had been getting ready to transport Evelyn's body to the medical examiner when one of the nurses heard the sound of the life support machine beeping. *I must have inadvertently forgotten to turn it off*, she thought to herself, but she heard another beep and then another and another.

The doctors and nurses rushed to Evelyn's room with great wonder and excitement. After confirming that she indeed was back from the dead, they called for Jeff and the girls.

Evelyn opened her eyes to see her husband choking back his tears. Then she found her girls, only this time for real. Adeline and Victoria stood beside the bed, holding her hand. Evelyn now knew that she was alive again. Turning toward them, she said, "Girls, what just happened?"

Victoria replied, "Momma, Adeline and I have not stopped praying for you since the minute we found out what happened."

"Girls," said Evelyn, "the strangest thing happened; both of you were with me, holding my right hand while Death was pulling my left hand toward him. That was the worst dream of my life."

Victoria, with tears streaming down her cheeks, said, "Momma, it wasn't a dream. You died but came back to life."

Evelyn responded, "Well, even if I died, I know that I had some type of dream of something." As she thought a little more, she asked Victoria, "Have you written a new song recently?"

"Why yes," said her daughter, "but Momma, how did you know? I haven't told anyone."

Evelyn looked up at her girls and grinned for a moment before she said innocently, "God is behind all of this, isn't He?"

Before the girls could respond, the cardiologist walked in and placed his stethoscope on one side of Evelyn's chest to check her heart.

"Evelyn, we thought we lost you; in fact, we did a few times. You are one fortunate woman. Is there anything we can get for you?"

Evelyn motioned for the doctor to come closer. He bent down as Evelyn raised up and whispered in his ear, "Yes, I need a Bible!"

Connecting "Spiritual Dots"

Hello, my name is Tom Covino. I'm not an entertainer, nor any kind of famous athlete or special person. I'm just like you, a human being trying to find his place in the world.

I have listened to many of the same songs you've listened to, watched a lot of the same movies, and have enjoyed playing and following my favorite athletes in their respective sports.

I am hoping that what you just read will cause you to pause for just a second to ask yourself this:

Why does man write so many songs and movies about our fast-approaching moment of death?

Why do we, as listeners, place such a premium on the songs we listen to and the movies we watch? Is it the cherished memories that bring us back to someone from our past or to someone in our future?

As life moves along swiftly, we seem to live our lives on some kind of stage, knowing that one day, the final curtain closes on us all in death.

Is there anyone or anything behind the curtain? Or…has man written these songs, penned their scripts about life and death simply for entertainment purposes and to pass the time?

The answer is summed up in one Bible verse, "Also, he has put eternity into man's heart" (Ecclesiastes 3:11). Who is He? Almighty God!

The Five Dots That Connected Me to the Truth Contained in the Bible, God's Word

The 1st Dot: I was a young boy of eight who needed to know why I was having these terrifying dreams about dying and being placed in a casket, put under the earth, with my eyes open, not knowing if I was dead or alive.

The 2nd Dot: At age twenty-one, I was playing a game of Trivial Pursuit with my girlfriend and a few friends one evening. I was about to win the game as Cyndee looked at my final question and frowned, knowing how easy it was.

The question was, "What are the first three words in the Bible?"

I can still remember the sinking feeling to this day as I delayed responding to Cyndee's question. I remember looking at her and thinking, *She's going to break up with me if I don't get this right!*

After about a minute or so, I blurted out my answer, "In the beginning?"

The group yelled out, "That's right!" followed by, "You were just messing with us, weren't you?"

The fact is, I wasn't messing with them. I didn't know. But somewhere or somehow, over the years, I must have heard it and stored this small truth away in a secret place.

The 3rd Dot: At age thirty-two, I had two jobs. The first was as an assistant golf professional, making very little money. The second was bartending at night at a small local pub in Sea Cliff, New York. It was at the pub "Costello's" that I met three regular customers.

Through each one of them, I began to see the real me. My life was like a movie stuck on a reel. It was the same script night after night, hearing the same songs on the jukebox and the same stories from those who ordered the same drink night after night.

While I thought that these three were the lonely people whom others talked about, the truth is, I knew that I was the loneliest of all. I just happened to be sitting on the other side of the bar where no one suspected.

One night, somewhere around 4 a.m., after I had closed the bar and after thinking that I had had enough of life on this certain stage, I stood outside my apartment, looked up at the sky, and screamed, "Is this what You created me for? To clean up after drunk people? If You're real, do something in my life!"

The Fourth Dot: Only nine months later, I moved to San Antonio, Texas, where I interviewed for another golf job and met the head professional, Mike Richards.

He asked me to hit a couple of golf shots, which I did. Without warning, he asked me, "Tom, are you saved?"

"Saved from what?" I answered.

"Tom, are you going to heaven?" he asked.

"I'm Roman Catholic, but not practicing." My head was down.

Five days later, Mr. Richards asked to see me again and said, "Congratulations, Tom, you're my new first assistant."

Although I needed the job badly, there was something much more important on my mind.

"Mr. Richards, can you please tell me what you meant by 'being saved'?"

He reached down behind the counter and handed me a Bible. Mr. Richards told me where to start reading at the beginning, which said, "In the beginning, God created the heavens and the earth" (Genesis 1:1).

My life would never be the same!

I sincerely hope that your life will never be the same after reading part two of this book.

I want to give you a fair warning about what you are about to read. While songs and movies leave a lasting impression upon our minds, some of the pictures you're about to see are designed for one thing and one thing only: your soul's well-being!

The 5th Dot: About two years ago, I watched the actual video of the conversation that actress Amanda Peet really had on Stephen Colbert's late-night talk show. It was at that time that God put it into my heart to write what you are reading right now.

I felt this overwhelming sense of urgency, thinking, *If Amanda could say that she feared death in front of the world, then I needed to do what I could to help her and as many others as I could, especially since I had lived in this fear all of my life prior to becoming a Christian.*

Do you remember Paul Revere's cry? "The redcoats are coming, the redcoats are coming!"

Amanda Peet shouting to the world, "I fear death," is because deep inside, she has a God-given conscience that has now been activated like a fire alarm that says, "The judgment of God is coming, the judgment of God is coming." This is fear that all humanity feels but often covers up, not wanting to face it head-on.

When One of the World's Dots Connects to One of God's, It is powerful to the soul:

World statistics say the life expectancy is 70.6 for men and 75.1 for women.

God says in the Bible:

"The years of our life are seventy, or even by reason of strength eighty" (Psalm 90:10).

The Four Dots Explained

They stand for the letters U, R, E, S.

The right script becomes…the right Scriptures—the Bible.

We all live our lives thinking we have the right script when, in fact, it falls short by four of the most important dots of your life: God's Scriptures. We live so close to the truth that God even says in the Bible, "They should seek God, in the hope that they might feel their way toward him and find him. Yet he is actually not far from each one of us" (Acts 17:27).

Mankind is so painstakingly close to the answer that brings the greatest joy, freedom, and hope, and yet so far. How far, you ask?

As far as their desire is to find out.

In the final part of this book, I will reveal seven doors, called the "Seven Doors of Death." You will see a picture and a scripture on each one. Upon walking through each door, you'll be escorted into a room that not only brings up what's on our minds but also the three areas of life that touch us the most: memories, regrets, and the hiding spot.

My end goal is to say and show you enough that you would open God's Word, the Bible, and see what has been shown to so many souls that have come and gone.

I'll also quote some of the most iconic entertainers of the past fifty years concerning their own mortality and their personal shouts for relief. These shouts come from the place that God most certainly placed inside each one of us when we were born—eternity in our hearts!

The question of questions is, "What happens to *you* when *you* die?"

Part 2: It Is Not A Game

The Seven Doors of Death

DOOR 1

PHYSICAL DEATH

"The BODY without the SOUL is DEAD!"
(James 2:26)

Doorway 1

This picture says it all. She could be Evelyn from *Jeopardy!* or your own mother. There we are, the family and friends standing outside the doorway desperately wanting to help, praying, giving her encouraging words, or simply standing there next to her for comfort.

What's going on in our minds and in hers?

Researchers say that we have 50,000 thoughts per day, but on a day like this, there's only one: death!

How uncomfortable is it for us to watch the life of anyone slowly slipping away? How much worse do you suppose it is for the one lying there in the bed, wondering what it's like to take their last breath, especially not knowing what comes next? For us who remain, it is the funeral.

The Funeral

It all begins when we arrive at the funeral home. After parking the car, we begin the slow walk to the door we least want to get to. We are greeted by a staff member who politely asks us for the last name. Upon giving it, she says, "Down the hall to your left."

In just a few seconds, we will join those who have made the walk and have entered the place we least desire. Before going in, we sign the guest book, pick up a picture of the deceased we've come to say goodbye to, and ready ourselves to enter the room.

The mental process begins upon entering the room. Much depends on the deceased's age, as well as our relationship with them. Most of us ignore the farthest place from where we entered the room, where the casket is, not yet ready to take our first glimpse of the truth. Our eyes now give approval; they take a quick look from afar. It is true; they really are gone.

Locking eyes with someone familiar, we politely nod and smile without bringing too much attention to ourselves. Scanning the room, we think to ourselves, *That must be the pastor or priest up in the front.* We take note of it to determine what kind of funeral is about to occur.

After taking our seats and hearing the soft music, our eyes see the revolving pictures just above and to the left of the one lying there motionless. Our hearts and minds are now fully engaged.

As the officiating minister offers a few opening words and a prayer, it is now official. From this point on, we are hearing about someone we once knew and that someone has died. The first wave of emotion hits us the hardest as we try to process the reality of it.

The speaker's responsibility is enormously important. He must convey a certain sentiment that brings us, as listeners, the most comfort and hope. The obituary is read, which begins with their name, where they were born, the day they died, and the many family members they left behind. Both family and friends are asked to participate in a short talk or to read a scripture. While we sit and listen to their life's story, the tears and the smiles find their way in.

Some forty-five minutes or so later, it's over, but it's not; it has only just begun. The final viewing line forms. Two more difficult moments to get through. The first one is taking a last look at their body. We aren't taught how to do this, so we look at the ones who have gone before us to figure out how long to stand there. Can we touch their hand? Should we pray?

We don't want to stand there too long and make a scene, yet not wanting to move along too fast and appear not to care enough. There's no script for this act of final viewing, but there are the most uncomfortable few seconds of silence as we walk away from the casket and up to the first person we speak to next, hopefully, someone we know.

When it comes to death and the funeral, we never know what is going to come out of our mouths. "They looked good, didn't they?" In a millisecond, we think, *Did I just really say that?* The person we said it to understands and feels the same way, and yet if we're both honest with ourselves, we would eventually admit that way down deep in our souls, there are so many questions we want to ask, but they stay locked away.

Now, a second line forms. We cringe inside, trying to rehearse what to say to the grieving family. If they were a great-grandparent to a friend of ours, well, it's not as bad as we thought. We think to ourselves and quickly offer to them when we get there something like "They had a wonderful long life," even convincing ourselves that death has just taken its natural course. After all, they were seventy-five and lived a good life with many beautiful memories.

However, if the person who died was someone young, whom you knew from high school, this can be the worst possible line you ever go through.

For this writer, back when I was seventeen, two of my classmates, Mike and Karen, died in a car crash, and their funerals were together. While I'm sure that most, if not all, of my classmates attended that day, I could not go and look death in the eye. The fear of death as a young boy kept me hiding and terrified to see a lifeless body.

While sudden memories of people from our past pop up, we are suddenly pulled back into the funeral we are currently attending. One of the staff members, trained in the language of professional compassion, announces that the service has ended. Maybe that's what he or she thought, but we know better. There's still the worst part to come.

The Gravesite

Now, back in our cars, we become part of the funeral procession, being led toward the cemetery. We are able to take a long collective breath as we watch the rest of the motorists around us give Death the right of way.

The ride is slow, but we eventually get there and begin a

second walk we would rather not take. The deafening silence has its grip on us all. Truly, no one is talking. The worst, most uncomfortable part of the funeral is the finality of it all.

The image of the pallbearers is a lasting one, three on one side and three on the other. They are carrying the person we once loved, admired, and shared so many memories with. How do we say goodbye when we believe we will never say hello again?

Daring to look around, we see two things: tears and blank stares. The preacher speaks with a sense of confidence toward the family in mourning before all goes silent again. Our last moment of getting close is placing a flower on their casket.

It all ends with the worst part of all, seeing their body go into the ground!

Death Statistics: 155,000 people die daily around the globe.

We become increasingly aware of time when we think about our mortality.

Long-time entertainer Woody Allen—actor, director, screenwriter, and four-time Academy Award winner—said this about dying, "Somewhere around five or so, I turned grumpier. When I became aware of my mortality, I didn't like the idea. You mean it ends? Deal me out! I don't want to play this game!"

Underneath our masks we are all aware of time.

The Inner Clock

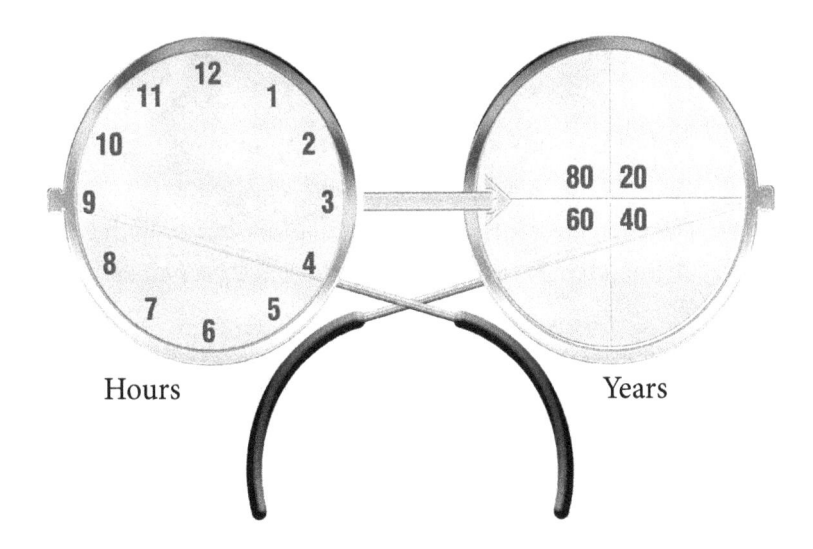

Hours   Years

0 - 20
"I can't wait 'til I grow up."

20 - 40
"You're getting old."

40 - 60
"I wish I was younger."

60 - 80
"What happens next?"

How terrible must it be for Mr. Allen, who lives day by day with the idea that it's just a matter of time before his number is called, and he's been living with that fear for over eighty years.

Mr. Allen starred with Diane Keaton in a 1975 movie called *Love and Death*. Perhaps through this movie, we get a glimpse of how people deal with death: humor.

At the end of the movie, there is an intriguing conversation between Boris (Allen) and Sonya (Keaton) as she looks through an open window and sees Boris standing next to a figure with a white sheet over his head, carrying a sickle, otherwise known as Death.

Sonya says, "Boris, what happened?"

Boris replies, "Some vision came and said that I was going to be pardoned, but then they shot me."

"You were my one great love!"

"Oh, thank you very much, I appreciate that! Now, if you'll excuse me, I'm dead."

"What's it like?"

"What's it like? You know the chicken at Trevski's?"

"Yes"

"It's worse!"

As Sonya closes the window after saying her goodbye, Boris, or maybe it really was Woody Allen, turns to the camera for a summary of his existence, "The question is, have I learned anything about life? Only that human beings are divided into mind and body. The mind embraces all the nobler aspirations, like poetry and philosophy, but the body has all the fun. The important thing, I think, is not to be bitter. You know, if it turns out that there is a God, I don't think that He's evil. I think that the worst you could say about Him is that, basically, He's an underachiever! After all, there are worse things in life than death! I mean, if you've ever spent an evening with an insurance salesman, you know exactly what I mean. The key here, I think, is not to think of death as an end, but think of it more as a very effective way of cutting down on your expenses."

With that, Boris (Woody Allen) is seen prancing and twirling together with Death alongside a small lake and a row of trees.

Could it be that Mr. Allen's character in the movie is his way of coping with the fear that has gripped him since he was five? To avoid playing the game that he wants to be dealt out of, he makes death a not-too-serious thing and God to be an underachiever.

Woody Allen's not alone in his fear.

Sadly, Death snatched a few other iconic figures in 2021: two of the nation's most influential radio and TV hosts, Larry King from CNN and Rush Limbaugh.

Interestingly enough, before he died, Mr. King was the one interviewed on the topic of death. Here's what he had to say, "I can't stand the thought of non-existence. You see, I already have existence!" Larry King died on January 23, 2021.

Do you remember the name "Hannibal Lecter"? Most people who recognize that name remember it before recognizing the actor who played him, Sir Anthony Hopkins.

In the movie *Silence of the Lambs*, one of Hollywood's best actors, Sir Anthony Hopkins, played a psychopath who abducts young and innocent women, first scaring them to death before actually murdering them.

Have you ever wondered if playing such a part in a movie like this has some residual effects on his perception of dying?

In a one-on-one interview with none other than his good friend, Larry King (of all people), he asked Hopkins, "Do you ever think about death?"

The superstar actor became vulnerable enough to remove part of his mask, "I think about death every day!"

This inner clock that makes us keenly aware of our mortality, which God has placed within all of us, sounds an alarm when we least expect it, and when it does, the reactions to the very thought of dying and our responses come from a hefty dose of truth serum within us all.

After two East Street Band members passed away, the legendary rock singer Bruce Springsteen found himself in an unusual place. "Depression isn't a gray sky. It's no color at all. I don't want to see tomorrow—what's the point of life? It's futile."

Bruce Springsteen has money, fame, and fortune but isn't satisfied with his life!

That is the conundrum we all find ourselves in.

The first step toward understanding the end of life is peeling back the mask of doubt, fear, and confusion to admit that we don't have all the answers until we ask the right questions. Bruce did ask the most important question on behalf of us all, "What's the point of living?"

However, because his answer is "futile," everything that he has accomplished feels unsatisfying, like having an unknown hole in the middle of him. Remember the first line to the song by Lady Gaga and Bradley Cooper?

It began with a question to a restless young man who was always trying to fill some kind of void in his life.

Bruce isn't alone in this world. Two anonymous men said, "Both my grandparents and parents have passed away…I feel like it's my turn next…like the batter in a baseball game who waits in the on-deck circle for his turn at bat. It's a horrible feeling."

A father called me (while writing this book) personally, saying, "My twelve-year-old daughter is petrified to go to sleep because she's afraid she won't wake up."

Mankind contemplates or suppresses daily just how long our

lifetime is. Or in the case of Anthony Hopkins, he thinks about death every day.

Is it any wonder?

It's hard not to think about death when we are constantly bombarded by reports of deaths that are occurring all around us. When we turn on CNN, Fox, or our local news in the city we live in and hear that another person has died from COVID-19, a sudden heart attack, or having succumbed to a long battle with cancer, it is a constant reminder.

Yet, sometimes, we are our own worst enemies. After a hard day's work, many of us retreat to our televisions just hoping to wind down, so we turn on *20/20*, *Dateline*, *Law and Order*, or one of the other shows that are supposed to entertain us. Instead, they become more reminders of what's really going on around us—people dying in every possible way, including seeing ourselves or mankind at its absolute worst, hating and taking lives!

Did you know? The Bible tells us about the world's first murder? "Cain spoke to Abel, his brother, and when they were in the field, Cain rose up against his brother Abel and killed him" (Genesis 4:8).

Can you imagine how their parents, Adam and Eve, felt? Their oldest son just murdered their youngest. They had never seen a lifeless body before, let alone their own precious sons. Is it any different today?

The Movie "Saving Private Ryan"

People in the movie theaters barely had enough time to settle in with their popcorn before being bombarded with our United States soldiers storming the beaches at Normandy in 1944 in the blockbuster movie *Saving Private Ryan*.

As the US Military boats approached the shoreline, the

intensity of the moment was seen on the men's faces as they crouched down. With the sound of the propellers beneath them and the eerie silence of intense anticipated machine gun fire about to begin, *fear* in the midst of their duty was seen.

In our humanity and in the conscience that we have been born with, no amount of training can withstand the fear that each soldier is only one bullet away from meeting his maker.

As they approached the shoreline, men were puking over the side of the boat; others had their heads down, with their eyes closed, silently praying. Jackson, who consistently referenced the Almighty God, kissed the cross he had around his neck.

In the theater, you could hear the sounds of grown men crying with each and every bullet finding the next soldier. The medic, played by Giovanni Ribisi, who was doing his best to heal the wounds of others, suddenly found himself at death's door. What did we hear him say as he lay there dying? "Momma, Momma," before he took his last breath.

Hollywood star Matt Damon, who seemed to have more than nine lives in the Jason Bourne series, was the one who played Ryan. In the end, with bombs bursting all around him, there's a closeup of his reaction to it all—he was human, with the only mouth God gave him; he sat frozen in fear, screaming at the top of his lungs.

As dedicated as every military man and woman is to their duty, the fear of dying is always close at hand.

In the end, I never thought that Hollywood would let one of its best, most beloved actors die, but they did. Tom Hanks died trying to save Private Ryan, and we all felt it together.

Four-Time Emmy-Award-Winning Television Show "This Is Us"

Has there ever been a more realistic show concerning the

memory and regret rooms, as well as our hiding spot?

This Is Us reminds us of what it's like to go back in time to recall our lives as children and how it has shaped our adult lives.

The acting is superb and as real as our tears and memories of being ushered back into both our memory and regret rooms.

The Pearsons, Jack and Rebecca, share their love story with the world. Though they come from polar opposite backgrounds, their bond is what we all yearn for. Rebecca (played by Mandi Moore) gives birth to twins Kevin and Kate; then, they adopt an abandoned African-American baby boy and name him Randall.

The Show Begins

Kevin, Kate, and Randall are introduced to us as adults who revisit their childhood past that has affected their current choices in life. Each one has his or her own triumphs and tragedies, all stemming from how they were raised. Kate fights a constant and worsening weight problem. Kevin, the jock actor, desperately looks for approval from his parents, often feeling neglected by them, causing him to have many problems with how to commit to a loving relationship.

Then there's Randall, who is successful and responsible but has deeper inner struggles resulting in panic attacks, having been left by his birth parents after being born. If that's not enough, the difficulty of fitting in with an all-white family and feeling different leads to all types of challenges. Although the father who adopted him, Jack, has been wonderful and loving to him, his incessant desire to know who his real father is has him on a long search for the truth.

Why is this show so popular?

The show is incredibly relatable. We know the best and worst of times in ourselves and others we come to know. We begin to feel its very name:

This Is Us becomes "This is me!"

For all of the Kates of the world who are self-conscious about the way we look to our peers, seeing her struggles connects us to her feelings. Whether it's our size, height, facial features, or something more, we all long to be accepted by others.

For all of us who see ourselves in Kevin, the athlete who needs to play a sport or an acting part well, someone who is driven to succeed but perhaps not for all the right reasons, we can relate in thinking that life is all about performing well to be loved.

For many, Randall's pain of feeling abandoned at birth, the void of an absent father, is so real, leading us into a mode of panic for most of our lives. Our fathers are everything. Living without their influence or not being close to them often leads us to a room that goes much deeper than the regret room. We find ourselves in the "hiding spot."

We Knew It Was Coming

When the writers and actors teased us with a trailer for the following week's episode. The strength of the show is based on family, the relationships, and the values that come with it.

What do the directors of this award-winning show know about us who watch each week? That we fall for the characters so much to the point of reliving our own lives through them.

Here is that episode that magnified our feelings for the Pearsons:

Kevin, Kate, and Randall are now teenagers sleeping in their comfortable beds, hours from waking up to the start of a normal day of life. Without any warning, smoke fills the house, and the first glimpses of fire are seen.

Jack, the ever-protecting father, would lead Rebecca and the children to safety. Yes, they would lose the physical things they had accumulated over time, but keeping the family alive was everything! When Kate is safely outside of the house, only then does she scream in horror that the dog is still inside. Like every other father watching the show that night, with this inherent devotion, driven by love and opportunity to protect his daughter's joy, Jack does the unthinkable by going back into the burning house to rescue Kate's dog.

I personally remember thinking to myself, *You can't have Jack die like this! It's too horrible of a picture in my mind to think about. Plus, you simply cannot have him die while having Jack save his daughter's pet. Or can you?*

Thankfully, the writers and actors got it right. Jack walks out with black on his face, covered with the effects of the smoke and fire, carrying Kate's dog. How the writers decide to start the Pearson's lives again is not on our minds. We only want to know that everyone made it out alive.

Expect the Unexpected

For precautionary matters, the family heads to the hospital to get checked by the doctors for smoke inhalation or any other possible injuries. The kids, being teenagers, are shaken up but physically okay.

In a private room, Jack and Rebecca are waiting for the doctor.

As expected, Jack is coughing a bunch, but nothing too alarming. Rebecca is strangely hungry and leaves in search of something to eat.

She finds a vending machine and begins to snack on a candy bar when the doctor comes in and says, "I'm sorry, Rebecca, Jack went into cardiac arrest."

Rebecca, with a confused look, pauses for a second before saying, "He's okay, right?"

As we watch in horror, waiting for a rewrite of the script, the doctor says to Rebecca, and to us all, having walked in her shoes, two of the most painful words a person can hear, "Jack died!"

Those of us who watched felt numb or shed a few tears, remembering someone who succumbed to the sting of death. Dying pushes us in many directions: shock, "It can't be true," followed by overwhelming grief and an instant thought, *They will never talk to us again.*

People we have loved and cared about for so many years end up in our hiding spots, where we ask that burning question, "Where are they now?"

No, really, where are they right now?

Prince, Princess Diana, Michael Jackson, Whitney Houston, Kobe Bryant, Robin Williams, Elvis Presley, John Lennon, Rush Limbaugh, your friend, my friend, our family members?

When we open the doors of our lives, many wonderful memories come flooding in. Unfortunately, there are plenty of regrets we must deal with as well, but there is also a room called the *hiding spot* that's reserved for keeping all to ourselves. Our personal secrets are kept there, including our own serious game of *Hide and Seek* with Death.

This door represents our minds

Do You Remember These Eight Decades of Life? (Time Flies, Doesn't It?)

We remember our decades by the big impacts around us, but when it comes to our personal years of living, it's all about the "four quarters."

1st Quarter, From Birth to Twenty: Between birth and graduating high school, you store up the greatest amount of memories as a kid! Friends for life, vacations to be remembered for all time, followed by the many special holidays; Christmas most likely topping the list of special moments with your family. You begin to have an appreciation for the four seasons and how warm or cold you were when you did this or that.

Learning to drive was huge. Spending more time with friends and away from the house is natural, but you know that there is nothing like home. Except for the pressures of trying to decide how to live your life going forward, what college to go to, and the type of profession you want to pursue, all in all, life has very few problems or regrets…you're too young for that.

2nd Quarter, From Twenty to Forty: Graduating college, you can't wait to get on with life. You're ready to be on your own, making something of yourself. You've been raised by Mom and Dad to work hard and to go after what it is that you want to pursue. You find the right one to spend the rest of your life with and get married. When you see and touch your baby for the first time, you realize that life will never be the same again. You can't believe the amount of love you have stored up in your heart, always ready to give to your children. Have you ever wondered where that love comes from?

3rd Quarter, From Forty to Sixty: You probably said to your friends, "I'm never going to be that old!" And now you are. The only way you remember what life was like between forty and fifty is by what your kids were doing or what was going on at work.

Up pops the first gray hair and then a wrinkle or two. Some begin losing their hair (and their confidence) as a friend who notices throws a jab or two their way.

The aches and pains of life begin to creep in. The first of several medications are prescribed for the beginning of high blood pressure or insomnia. Perhaps you have your first blood test in a while that shows that the inside of your body isn't looking like your outside. You see your first heart doctor, and they tell you to change your lifestyle. Concerned for the moment, you place it in your "hiding spot."

There's a softening to you that is seen with each familiar song, bringing you back to the first quarter of life. With each smell that has burned into your brain and each lyric that reminds you of someone special, you long for those moments to be recaptured, yet know it's not possible. When the song ends, or you blow out the candle, you are quickly escorted back to the truth, which is that there's no going back…only time speeding ahead.

4th Quarter, From Sixty to Eighty: You will never be able

to blow out fifty-nine candles again because you will always be greater than sixty for the rest of your days. You stuff that away as you play with your grandchildren. You travel because you have retired. You don't sleep as well, feel tired too often, and wonder if a major sickness is heading your way. More of your high-school friends have passed away.

Within each of these four quarters, the very best memories of life have two effects on us: one that says, "I'd like to add a few more," and two, "One day soon, I won't have any more!"

And then it hits us—some more than others. What once was a life full of memories is now reduced to forgetting names, times, places, and seasons. We are nearing the end, and there's not a thing anyone can do but remember for you.

Overtime: Eventually, death will score, and the game of life will be over. As Tom Brady said to a reporter who asked him why he was leaving the New England Patriots, "Everything must come to an end!"

We are nearing the end of life, and there is not a thing anyone can do to stop it.

When our life ends here, it takes us to door number 2.

> **JUDGMENT AFTER DEATH**
>
> *"And just as It is appointed for man to die once, and after that comes judgment."*
> (Hebrews 9:27)
>
> DOOR 2

Doorway 2

Why are we enslaved to the fear of death? Because not only has God "put eternity in our hearts," but He also says, "All have sinned and fall short of the glory of God!" (Romans 3:23).

This is what our fear is all about!

The Courtroom

As you walk through this door, you need to picture a courtroom scene with all of mankind sitting on the left side of the room…all are sitting on the left, and no one is on the right.

When we die, we end up on the left side of the judge who has not yet taken His seat, but when He gets there, He will pronounce you, me, all of us guilty.

All the GOATs in every industry are present: including Jeff Bezos, Bill Gates, and Elon Musk, to name a few.

All of the presidents you and I grew up listening to and voting for will sit on the left side of judgment. We will remember those who served in office in our lifetime.

Those who grew up in the '40s and are still alive in the '20s have seen the leading authority of Franklin Roosevelt, Truman, Eisenhower, JFK, LBJ, Nixon, Ford, Carter, Reagan, Bush 1, Clinton, Bush 2, Obama, Trump and our current one, President Biden.

They got to the top of the United States of America; they were and still are the GOATs we remember as someone who did their best to lead a nation of people in a land that sits on a small portion of the earth that sits effortlessly in space.

At the judgment, how they served the people of the United States and what they are remembered for, good and bad, will have no bearing before God.

All are sitting on the left! Can you see it?

Being a famous actor, singer, or athlete, while it has its enjoyment and rewards, will have no bearing after death.

Oprah, Mark Cuban, Mr. Wonderful (Kevin O'Leary), and the rest of the sharks on *Shark Tank*. Drake, Tupac Shakur, Blake Shelton, George Strait, Madonna, Eminem, Robert Downey Jr., Tom Cruise, Tom Holland, Brad Pitt, Adele, Lady Gaga, Tiger Woods, Tom Brady, LeBron James, Wayne Gretzky, and of course, John Lennon, and many others, along with their songs, movies, games, and their lives will have come to an end.

On the left, sitting there after death, will be every type of person, like the ones we saw in the movie *Titanic*. There were three types of passengers in life!

First Class

Second Class

Third Class

In the movie, as the Titanic was going down, Jack (Leonardo DiCaprio), Rose (Kate Winslet), and one of the ship's chefs or bakers were hanging onto the last part of the back of the ship as it went down into the Atlantic. The three represent anyone who is rich (Rose), middle class (Baker), and poor (Jack).

Do you remember how the three types reacted just after the Titanic hit the iceberg?

The lower-class passengers, those with the least amount of money, who stayed on the lower deck of the ship, felt the sting of the icy water and quickly began running up to safety.

A few of the middle-class passengers were playing soccer with some of the iceberg pieces that fell on the ship, acting as if it wasn't a big deal.

Then there were the rich, who were scripted to say, "I'd like a cup of tea waiting for me in my room when I get back."

While just a movie, we can know for sure that fame, athletic ability, education, economic status, color, and what part of the world we live in will not matter in the end; what matters is what side of the courtroom we are sitting on.

We will all be in these seats together, yet we can't help one another. Like the Titanic, each one of us personally hit the iceberg when we sinned against God. We are now personally responsible for our own death. So, we find ourselves sitting on the left side of the courtroom, waiting for sentencing.

Suddenly, above the judge's chair, this pops up for all to see:

"For the wages of sin is death!" (Romans 6:23).

This question comes to your mind. "Hey, I'm dead and sitting in a courtroom that says I've died because I've sinned?"

Then someone sitting next to you says, "That's not what He's saying at all. Yes, we have died physically because we have sinned, but there's still a sentencing we have to go through."

May I say this to you now? Go quickly to the Bible!

God says, "We all sin and fall short of His expectations, and the consequence of this is death!" How awful is that?

"What kind of death?" you question in your mind. There are two kinds:

One: Physical, "Just as through one man [Adam] sin entered into the world, and death through sin, and so death spread to all men because all sinned" (Romans 5:12).

Two: Spiritual, "They will pay the penalty of eternal destruction away from the presence of the Lord" (2 Thessalonians 1:9).

Many in the world will say, "God, I was a good person."

And God will say, "None is righteous no, not one, no one seeks for God, all have turned aside, together they have become worthless; no one does good not even one" (Romans 3:10–12).

Many others might say, "I didn't know."

And God will say, "For what can be known about God is plain to them, because God has shown it to them. For his invisible attributes, namely, his eternal power and divine nature, have been clearly perceived, ever since the creation of the world, in the things that have been made, so they are without excuse" (Romans 1:20).

Please pick up your Bible, I beg you!

God's eternal power can be read on the first page of the Bible, that in the beginning, He created the heavens and the earth. He also decided to "make man in His image."

If you pick up a Bible, you will read that "God is light, in Him is no darkness!" This means that God cannot lie but only speak the truth.

In your body and mine is a soul that searches for the truth about God before we die. But before we get there, let's hear what God says about us being born into this world.

King David said:

"I am fearfully and wonderfully made" (Psalm 139:14).

"You knitted me together in my mother's womb" (Psalm 139:13).

"For you formed my inward parts" (Psalm 139:13).

The prophet Jeremiah said:

"Before I formed you in the womb, I knew you" (Jeremiah 1:5).

King Solomon said:

"God made man upright, but they have sought out many schemes" (Ecclesiastes 7:29).

What we are staring at in our fear of death is God's truth to man about his birth from the beginning. It's all from God. God knew each one of us before our souls were placed in a baby's body. Yet the sad fact is that while God made man upright and a blessing for all parents at their birth, that child will eventually seek out schemes and commit sins against our loving and holy God.

These next three verses tell us what happens after death:

"All are from the dust, and to the dust all return" (Ecclesiastes 3:20).

"And the dust returns to the earth as it was, and the spirit [soul] returns to God who gave it" (Ecclesiastes 12:7).

"For we will all stand before the judgment seat of God" (Romans 14:10).

Did You See the Movie "The Fly"?

In the movie, a scientist trying to tweak the natural order of man and insects decides to conduct an experiment, which, in the end, causes his human head and face to be on the body of a small fly.

At the end of the movie, this man-fly has found himself stuck in a spider's web near the bottom of a park bench, unable to move. As he sees the spider approaching, he lets out the highest scream possible, yet he is unable to be heard because of his small size.

As a woman decides to sit on the very bench above him, she faintly hears him, looks down, and sees the spider only a few inches from his prey. As the spider lunges and the man screams, she picks up a rock, killing them both instantly.

Mankind lives like a fly caught in a web. Since God has put eternity into man's heart, which allows us to instinctively know that after we die, we will stand before the judgment seat of God, it's only natural or expected that we feel trapped like a fly.

Do You Have Trouble Believing in God?

The Bible says, "The fool says in his heart, 'There is no God'" (Psalm 14:1).

This is why everyone in the world sitting on the left side of the courtroom feels helpless and hopeless like the fly, and it explains the gripping fear that you have felt or still feel.

Listen to some of the voices of those who were and are caught in the web of fear:

"I fear everything, and it's much worse than that" (Robin Williams).

"I hate the thought of non-existence, you see, I already have existence" (Larry King).

Both have died! Both found out the truth the moment they took their last breath!

Now, picture yourself or someone else in the courtroom standing up and shouting, "I fear death! I need to know what to believe in! I don't want to be a bag of dust!"

There she is, Amanda Peet, telling the world, "I'm afraid, but I no longer want to be. Can anyone help me?" The answer is "Yes" because Amanda Peet is *still alive*…thank God!

Is she alone? No! While you have not yet died, you have thought about it, I'm sure, and God says so.

Can you picture the view on the left side of the courtroom? Can you envision the gavel? It's the gavel that says guilty of sin! It's where sinners will sit, on the left.

The worst part of living is when the fear of dying comes into view and the feeling that we will take our place on the left without any hope.

All of mankind's pleas feel like the name of this book, *Dear God, My Life's in Jeopardy*, because it's the moment that a soul cries out to be right with God, knowing that the danger of judgment or the Final Jeopardy moment has arrived.

Do you want to hear the good news? It's only a matter of your soul believing what you are about to read on the next page and enter door number 3. But it begins with the ten most important words ever spoken to the human soul:

"Father, forgive them, for they know not what they do" (Luke 23:34).

I now invite you to come closer to door number 3. Please let the words that are written on this door and what you will read next be the ultimate moment of truth for your soul to receive:

Doorway 3

"I am the resurrection and the life. Whoever believes in me, though he die, yet shall he live" (John 11:25).

Question: Do you know what is keeping you alive today?

Answer: It's the blood that circulates inside your body!

Question: Do you know what keeps a soul living for all eternity?

Answer: The blood of His cross!

"For in him [Jesus Christ] all the fullness of God was pleased to dwell, and through him [Jesus Christ] to reconcile to himself all things, whether on earth or in heaven, making peace by the blood of his cross" (Colossians 1:20).

"Without the shedding of blood, there is no forgiveness of sins" (Hebrews 9:22).

"But God shows his love for us that while we were still sinners, Christ died for us. Since therefore we have been justified by his blood, much more shall we be saved by him from the wrath of God" (Romans 5:8, 9).

As for man's fear of death?

"That through death he [Jesus] might destroy the one who has the power of death, that is, the devil [T. D.] and deliver all those who through fear of death were subject to lifelong slavery" (Hebrews 2:15).

What does this mean?

The *only* way for a man's soul to be at peace and innocent before God after he dies and goes to judgment is through the death and blood of Jesus Christ that was shed for the remission of our sins.

Listen to what He did for us, "But he was wounded for our transgressions; he was crushed for our iniquities; upon him was the chastisement that brought us peace, and with his stripes we are healed. All we like sheep have gone astray; we have turned every one to his own way, and the LORD has laid on him the iniquity of us all" (Isaiah 53:5–6).

Before a single nail was struck into his wrists and feet that day, the soldiers "Stripped him and put a scarlet robe on him, and twisting together a crown of thorns, they put it on his head and put a reed in his right hand. And kneeling before him, they mocked him, saying, 'Hail King of the Jews!' And they spit on him and took the reed and struck him on the head. And when they had mocked him, they stripped him of the robe and put his own clothes on him and led him away to crucify him" (Matthew 27:28–31).

Before Jesus died on the cross and shed His blood for the

forgiveness of sins, a long, long time ago, God told Moses to tell the Israelites who were in slavery to the pharaoh in the land of Egypt to "Go and select lambs for yourselves and kill the Passover lamb. Take a bunch of hyssop and dip it in the blood and touch the lintel and the two doorposts with the blood that is in the basin. None of you shall go out of the door of his house until the morning. For the LORD will pass through to strike the Egyptians and when he sees the blood on the lintel and the two doorposts, the LORD will pass over the door and will not allow the destroyer to enter your houses to strike you" (Exodus 12:21–23).

Here is the spiritual connecting dot between the Old and New Testament; as John the Baptist said, "Behold the Lamb of God who takes away the sins of the world."

"For Christ, our Passover lamb, has been sacrificed. Therefore let us celebrate…" (1 Corinthians 5:7–8).

God's Son spilled His perfect, righteous blood on the cross. Whoever believes in Jesus enough to follow Him will have the righteous blood of Christ placed on the doorposts of their unrighteous souls. When this happens, God, on judgment day, will pass over every single one of your sins.

May that day happen when it hits you strong enough to think or say, "God took my sins and placed them on His Son's body, resulting in the ultimate punishment, the cross!"

Can you imagine? Your soul justified in the sight of the Creator of the world? Being washed in the blood of the God who loves you? Wanting you to know a peace that surpasses all understanding? To be saved from the punishment that should be yours but isn't? And that your name is now written in the Lamb's Book of Life, heaven?

Now that you know this…

God makes this statement once again through the apostle Paul. It was to a group of religious people trying to find out who God was.

> Men of Athens, I perceive that in every way you are very religious. For as I passed along and observed the objects of your worship, I found also an altar with this inscription: "To the unknown god." What you worship as "unknown," this I proclaim to you. The times of ignorance God overlooked, but now he commands all people everywhere to repent, because he has fixed a day on which he will judge the world in righteousness by a man whom he has appointed; and of this he has given assurance to all by raising him from the dead.
>
> Acts 17:22–23, 30–31

It is silly to believe in and follow a dead man unless that dead man is alive!

Here is what Jesus Christ is offering you today, right now, as you see the billions of people on the left side of the courtroom, which may include you who are reading this.

"I am the way, the truth and the life. No one comes to the Father except through me" (John 14:6).

Hearing God's Word will produce one of three reactions: faith, mocking, or delaying.

"Now when they heard of the resurrection of the dead, some mocked, but others said, 'We will hear you again about this.' But some men joined him and believed, and a woman named Damaris and others with them" (Acts 17:32–34).

Sadly, but honestly, God tells us in His Word, the Bible, "The word of the cross is folly to those who are perishing […] it pleased God through the folly of what we preach to save those who believe. For the Jews demand signs and the Greeks seek wisdom, but we preach Christ crucified, a stumbling block to Jews and folly to Gentiles" (1 Corinthians 1:18, 21–23).

Yet joyfully, this is said too, "But to us who are being saved it is the power of God!" (1 Corinthians 1:18).

Their hearts were enlightened. They heard God's Word, and it produced faith (Romans 10:17). And when that happens, this happens, "When one turns to the lord, the veil is removed [Only through Christ is it taken away]" (2 Corinthians 3:16). Removing the veil means that a person can suddenly see and hear the truth. And when that happens, a common question seems to come from the mouths of those who believe the truth about Jesus Christ.

When the church that Jesus died for first began, thousands heard the preaching of the apostle Peter (Acts Chapter 2).

When he finished, the crowd asked, "What shall we do?" (now that we believe).

Once you believe, as they did too, we invite you to door number 4… This is the *moment* your soul has been waiting for!

The following picture is of someone who is dying with Christ in baptism. This man is becoming a Christian because he has heard the message of the gospel and is obeying the command to repent and be baptized (immersed) in the name of Jesus Christ.

When he comes up out of the water, he will have been cleansed from all of his past sins in the powerful working of God and escorted from the left to the right side of the courtroom where only the innocent sit.

DOOR 4

BELIEVER'S DEATH

"Do you not know that all of us who have been baptized into Christ Jesus have been baptized into His death..."
Romans 6:3

Doorway 4

After Jesus died and was resurrected, He came to Jerusalem to show Himself alive to the apostles. His very first command to them, after He rose from the dead, was and still is so significant.

Jesus makes this statement:

"All authority in heaven and on earth has been given to me. Go therefore and make disciples of all nations, baptizing them in the name of the Father and of the Son and of the Holy Spirit, teaching them to observe all things that I have commanded you…" (Matthew 28:18–20).

What It Means to Make a Disciple

Though a passage like this is very straightforward, sometimes we need to hear it explained in a way that helps us better understand it.

Jesus is saying, "Tell and teach all people in every place where you go that I am the promised Messiah that Moses spoke about; that I am the Christ, the Son of the living God. Tell them how I died for them on the cross and that I took the punishment for their sins upon myself and tasted death for them. Tell them that I was, in fact, raised from the dead on the third day, just like what I had said. Tell them that you and over 500 others saw Me resurrected. Tell them about the centurion soldier who saw the darkness over the land from noon till 3 p.m., who declared, 'Truly, this was the son of God.' Tell them about the seven statements I made when I was hanging on that cross, especially My prayer on their behalf. 'Forgive them, Father, for they know not what they do.' If they believe you, baptize them [the Believer's Death] for the remission of their sins!"

The Believer's Death—The First 3,000 Conversions

The apostle Peter said, "Men of Israel, hear these words: Jesus of Nazareth, a man attested to you by God with mighty works and wonders and signs that God did through him in your midst, as you yourselves know—this Jesus, delivered up according to the definite plan and foreknowledge of God, you crucified and killed by the hands of lawless men. God raised him up, loosing the pangs of death because it was not possible for him to be held by it.

"Let all the house of Israel therefore know for certain that God has made him both Lord and Christ,

> this Jesus whom you crucified." Now when they heard this they were cut to the heart [they believed] and said to Peter and the rest of the apostles, "Brothers, what shall we do?"
>
> Acts 2:22–24, 36–38

Peter could have said, "You do not need to do anything now that you believe you are saved." He could've said to get down on your knees to pray and ask Jesus into your heart, or even to just confess that Jesus is Christ and you will be saved.

Peter said, "Repent and be baptized every one of you in the name of Jesus Christ for the forgiveness of your sins" (Acts 2:38).

The response from the crowd was, "So those who received his word were baptized, and there were added that day about three thousand souls" (Acts 2:41).

The Believers' Deaths—Men and Women

> Phillip [not an apostle] went down to the city of Samaria and proclaimed to them the Christ. And the crowds with one accord paid attention to what was being said by Phillip when they heard him […] when they believed Phillip as he preached good news about the kingdom of God and the name of Jesus Christ, they were baptized, both men and women.
>
> Acts 8:5–6, 12

The Believer's Death—The Ethiopian Eunuch

> An angel of the Lord said to Phillip, "Rise and

go toward the south to the road that goes down from Jerusalem to Gaza." This is a desert place. And he rose and went. And there was an Ethiopian, a eunuch, a court official of Candace, queen of the Ethiopians, who was in charge of all her treasure. He had come to Jerusalem to worship and was returning, seated in his chariot. And he was reading the prophet Isaiah. And the Spirit said to Philip, "Go over and join this chariot." So Philip ran to him and heard him reading Isaiah the prophet and asked, "Do you understand what you are reading?" And he said, "How can I, unless someone guides me?" And he invited Phillip to come up and sit with him. Now the passage of the scripture that he was reading was this:

"Like a sheep he was led to the slaughter and like a lamb before it's shearer is silent, so he opens not his mouth […]" And the Eunuch said to Philip, "About whom, I ask you, does the prophet say this, about himself or about someone else?"

Then Philip opened his mouth, and beginning with this Scripture he told him the good news about Jesus.

Acts 8:26–32, 34

By now, we have a pretty good idea of what preaching Jesus is. Philip made a disciple of a man who was already hungry for the truth. How do we know? By the very first statement, once Philip stopped preaching, "And as they were going along the road they came to some water, and the eunuch said, 'See, here is water! What prevents me from being baptized?'" (Acts 8:36).

Wow! Just like that, with preaching the simple message of the gospel, that Jesus was the Lamb of God that would take away his sins, the eunuch can't help but ask for water, not the water that would quench his physical thirst, but the water that could be used to quench his spiritual thirst for forgiveness. "And he commanded the chariot to stop, and they both went down into the water, Philip and the eunuch, and he baptized him" (Acts 8:38).

The eunuch's soul had experienced the believer's death, exactly how Jesus commanded it after being resurrected from the dead and meeting with the apostles, who in turn must have explained it to Philip.

Please note that the angel went to Philip and told him where to go. After he went, the Holy Spirit told Philip to join the chariot. I say this to say God could have sent an angel or the Holy Spirit directly to the eunuch to save him, but He didn't.

What was true then is still true today: "Faith comes by hearing and hearing by the word of God" (Romans 10:17).

God chose to have the message of the cross and salvation through Jesus Christ as the message that would cause souls to accept or reject the truth.

The Believer's Death—The Apostle Paul, Formerly Saul

> As I was on my way and drew near Damascus, about noon a great light from heaven suddenly shone around me. And I fell to the ground and heard a voice saying to me, "Saul, Saul, why are you persecuting me?" And I answered, "Who are you, Lord?" And he said to me, "I am Jesus of Nazareth, whom you are persecuting." And I said, "What shall I do Lord?" And he said to me, "Rise and go into Damascus and there you will be told all that is appointed for you to do."

Acts 22:6–8, 10

Saul is now a believer in the resurrected Jesus, a disciple who has learned the truth, albeit the hard way. Paul was blinded after seeing the glory of Jesus Christ. He had to be led into Damascus by those who were with him.

There is a big question we must ask now that Saul is a believer in the resurrected Christ, "Is he saved at this moment?" Apparently not, because God sent a man named Ananias to speak to him.

> And he said, "The God of our fathers appointed you to know his will, to see the Righteous One and to hear an utterance from his mouth, for you will be a witness for him to all men of what you have seen and heard. Now why do you delay? Get up and be baptized and wash away your sins, calling on his name."

Acts 22:14–16

Calling on the name of Jesus can't be by belief alone. God has always desired a faith that will obey. In the Gospel of Matthew, Jesus said, "Not everyone who says to me, 'Lord, Lord,' will enter the kingdom of heaven, but he who does the will of my Father who is in heaven will enter" (Matthew 7:21).

Question: What is baptism for?

The word "for" means "in order to," "toward," and "for the putting away."

When Peter told the people to repent and be baptized "for" the remission of sins, it was "in order to" have their sins removed. Please keep in mind that this was the very first sermon after Jesus was resurrected from the dead and after He met with the apostles and gave His first command, which included being baptized.

The Believer's Death—Lydia and Her Household

"The Lord opened her heart to pay attention to what was said by Paul. And after she was baptized, and her household as well, she urged us, saying, 'If you have judged me to be faithful to the Lord, come to my house and stay'" (Acts 16:14–15).

What a wonderful and easy conversion.

The Believer's Death—The Philippian Jailor

>About midnight, Paul and Silas were praying and singing hymns to God, and the prisoners were listening to them. And suddenly there was a great earthquake, so that the foundations of the prison were shaken, and immediately all the doors were opened, and everyone's bonds were unfastened. When the jailer woke up and saw that the prison doors were open, he drew his sword and was about to kill himself, supposing that the prisoners had escaped. But Paul cried with a loud voice, "Do not harm yourself, for we are all here."
>
>"And the jailer called for lights and rushed in, and trembling with fear he fell down before Paul and Silas. Then he [the jailer] brought them out and said, 'Sirs, what must I do to be saved?'"

Acts 16:25–30

There is that question again from a heart that's seeking, "Sirs, what must I do to be saved?" May I remind you what God says, "Faith comes by hearing and hearing by the word of God" (Romans 10:17).

Let's see what Paul did.

And they spoke the word of the Lord to him and to all who were in the house, we told him about Jesus. And he [the jailer] took them the same hour of the night and washed their wounds [repenting]; and he was baptized at once, he and all his family. And he rejoiced along with his entire household that he had believed in God.

Acts 16:32–34

Look at the Connecting Dots

1. They spoke the truth to the jailor.
2. His repentance was demonstrated by the washing of their wounds.
3. He and his family were baptized at once.

These three are connected to believing in God.

The believer's death then is the believer's death today.

I have no idea what you have been told before about God and salvation. I don't know if you have ever read the Bible before (I didn't until age thirty-three) or what your parents might have told you, but I do know this: after hearing a sermon from one of the apostles, people knew exactly what they needed to believe and do to be reconciled back to God.

Saving faith doesn't happen by chance; it is a collision of God's truth hitting man's heart.

God had the apostle Paul write this to the church of Rome:

> We have been buried with Him through baptism into

death, so that as Christ was raised from the dead through the glory of the father, so we too might walk in newness of life. For if we have become united with Him in the likeness of His death, certainly we shall also be in the likeness of His resurrection. Knowing this, that our old self was crucified with Him, in order that our body of sin might be done away with so that we may no longer be slaves to sin.

Romans 6:4–6

The believer's death is mentioned again and again.

"If with Christ you died…" (Colossians 2:20).

"For you have died…" (Colossians 3:3).

"If we died with him, we shall also live with him" (2 Timothy 2:11).

The question is, "When do we die with Christ?" The answer is, "When we are buried with Him in baptism!"

Some may argue that baptism isn't necessary for salvation because it would be a work of man.

The Bible tells us that it is actually a work of God!

"Having been buried with him in baptism, in which you were also raised with him through faith in the powerful *working of God* who raised him from the dead" (Colossians 2:12, author's italics).

One of the most emotional moments on this earth for two men:

John De La Rosa, in his seventies, walked up to his ninety-seven-year-old mother, who was lying in the casket. John had had the gospel preached to him for many years—almost fifty. Though many family members and friends talked to him about obeying the gospel, John just wasn't ready. But after seeing the stillness of his mother lying there, John's heart must have realized that he may not ever have another chance.

John summoned my brother-in-law and then me, saying, "I want to be baptized for the remission of my sins." With nineteen family members there to witness it, John De La Rosa, my father-in-law, got up from the left side of the courtroom and died with Christ in baptism. John lost his earthly life a year ago last May, exchanging it for an eternal life that lives forever.

My dad, Tom Covino, Sr., and I agreed to study the Bible. We talked about the Scriptures for over six months. He had many questions about the beliefs that he was raised with. With every question, there was a biblical answer. While visiting him in Tennessee, we were swimming in a local pool when he said, "I know that If I'm not baptized, I will be going to hell."

What a joy it was to baptize my dad that day and know that all of his sins were washed away because he believed in Jesus Christ. Again, only a few short years after that, my dad's body succumbed to his mortality, and he died. But he died in faith.

I am so encouraged for John De La Rosa and my father, Tom Covino, Sr. "Blessed are the dead who die in the Lord" (Revelation 14:13).

There's a spiritual "elephant" in the room.

Elephant

Have You Been Baptized Correctly, According to God's Will?

What I am about to say to you right now, I have prayed to God about.

The word for "baptize" in Greek is *baptizo* or *bapto*. It means to plunge, immerse, or overwhelm. The word *rantizo* in Greek means to sprinkle, and the word *cheo* in Greek means to pour.

I have searched the Scriptures concerning every time the word "baptism" is used. Not once are the words *rantizo* or *cheo* ever used.

At this point, I lovingly share this with all: according to the Bible, infant baptism *is not* baptism.

Wouldn't it be just like the god of this world (the devil) to try to cause confusion when it comes to baptism? He blinds the minds of those who do not believe (2 Corinthians 4:4).

We can be sure that when the eunuch suddenly cried out for water: "See, here is water! What prevents me from being baptized?" (Acts 8:36). After Philip preached Jesus to him, there could only be two possibilities regarding the water he was talking about.

So, either it just hit him that his "being in the desert" was referring to the water in some small pouch or container that he kept with him for when he was physically thirsty and now realized that there was enough in to have Philip sprinkle or pour the water on him, or the eunuch was shocked to see a large body of water. He shouted, "See, here is water!"

Fortunately for us, God doesn't leave us guessing. Here are the exact words from God's perfect Word, the Bible, "As they were going down the along road they came to some water, and the eunuch said, 'See, here is water! What prevents me from being baptized?'" (Acts 8:36). Then the Bible says, "They both went down into the water, Philip and the eunuch, and he baptized him"

(Acts 8:38). And if there was any shred of doubt, our minds can picture what is said next, "And when they *came up* out of the water" (Acts 8:39, author's italics).

We can now know that the believer's death by baptism (immersion) is carried out in a place that contains enough water to place a person's entire body underneath it.

One may think to ask, "Should it really matter how I was baptized? Shouldn't the most important thing be that I believe in God enough to be baptized and that maybe He doesn't care whether it was by immersion, sprinkling, or pouring?"

Let's let God tell us through His Word: "John was also baptizing in Aenon near Salim, because there was much water there" (John 3:23).

Not only is it important as to who is baptized and the amount of water necessary, but there is a third element that God has commanded for His followers, and that is to be baptized into the name of Jesus.

Here is the exchange of those who had been baptized into John's baptism to whom the apostle Paul asked, "Into what then were you baptized?" The disciples said, "Into John's baptism" (Acts 19:3).

Listen carefully to what Paul says next, "John baptized with the baptism of repentance, telling the people to believe in the One who was to come after him, that is, Jesus" (Acts 19:4).

The apostle Paul has just told them they need to be baptized again, this time in the name of Jesus. What's important to see is how the people responded that day. The Bible says, "Upon hearing this, they were baptized [immersed] in the name of the Lord Jesus" (Acts 19:5).

Baptism must be more important than we think if one man in the desert is so excited to see enough water to die with Christ and others have no dispute with the apostle Paul for being correctly baptized into the name of Jesus Christ. My dear reader, dying with Christ in baptism is when your sins are washed away. It's that important to the apostle Paul because he was inspired by God to tell them.

The reason I have chosen to title this door "The Believer's Death" is because of what is written by the apostle Paul in Romans 6:3, "Do you not know that all of us who have been baptized into Christ Jesus were baptized into His death?"

There are approximately 1.3 billion people on earth who believe and have confessed that Jesus is the Christ and were baptized (sprinkled or poured on) as babies, believing that they have obeyed God's command. If you are someone in this category like I was, I pray that you would take the time to read the Scriptures for yourself. Here is something that helped me, and I hope it will help you, too.

Whatever question you might have concerning your beliefs, if you pick up the Bible and look for every scripture having to do with the topic in question, letting go of anything and everything that you have been told before, God will reveal the truth to you on that topic.

Question: Why do many parents all over the world choose to baptize their precious babies?

Some misunderstand Luke 18:15, "Now they were bringing even infants to Him [Jesus] that He might touch them." In Matthew's account, "The children were brought to Him that He might lay His hands on them and pray" (Matthew 19:13). What did Jesus do? He touched them (to bless them), and He prayed for them. But not a single word about baptizing them.

Please consider this: the apostles were sometimes overly protective over Jesus's time because so many parents wanted Jesus to bless their babies. The word "bless" means to speak well of, to celebrate, to cause to prosper, and to make happy, to name a few.

Doesn't this sound about right? The words that our Lord Jesus said that day, "Permit the children to come to me, do not hinder them, for the kingdom of God belongs to such as these" (Matthew 19:4). He goes on to say, "Truly I say to you, whoever does not receive the Kingdom of God like a child shall not enter it" (Mark 10:15).

What does Jesus mean when He said to receive the kingdom of God like a child? It means to be humble and innocent as a baby, infant, or child.

May I ask you a question?

Do you believe that the moment that a baby leaves his or her mother's womb, they have sinned against God? Wouldn't we all agree that if that were so, the urgency for someone to quickly come in and rush the baby to a bathtub of water would make sense? Wouldn't we all, as sincere religious parents, have suddenly realized that our newborn blessing from God is now at odds with Him and again rushed the infant to the nearest pool of some sort?

As a former Catholic, I know that babies are typically baptized (sprinkled or poured on) in the first few weeks or months after they are born. Would loving parents who believe in baptism really wait so long to do something that forgives sins?

There is a well-known doctrine that came about in the sixteenth century that declared that every baby born into the world inherits the sin and guilt of Adam. This is called the doctrine of original sin.

Let's see what God has to say. Solomon, the wisest man who ever lived, to whom God gave the most incredible wisdom, said, "Lo, this only have I found, that God has made man upright [just and right] but they have sought out many schemes" (Ecclesiastes 7:29).

On the heels of that statement is this from King David, "For You formed my inward parts, You knitted me together in my mother's womb, for I am fearfully and wonderfully made, my soul knows it very well" (Psalm 139:13–14).

David says only wonderful things about how his soul knows that God had made him perfect (fearfully and wonderfully made) from the beginning.

Then comes the prophet Ezekiel, who says, "The soul who sins shall die. The son shall not suffer for the iniquity of the father" (Ezekiel 18:20).

If all babies sin at their birth, when did it happen? And if they did, then we would be blaming God for doing what David said, "You formed my inward parts, I am wonderfully and fearfully made" (Psalm 139:13–14).

There is nothing about Adam's sins being transferred to his first or second son's accounts. But as for the spreading of sins from person to person, let us be reminded of those powerful words that God gave to Ezekiel, "The soul that sins shall die" (Ezekiel 18:20). And not what man says, "The soul of the baby has sinned by being born." Our beautiful babies are just that, beautifully made by God, ordained by Him in the book of Genesis for Adam and Eve to start the process of mankind inhabiting the earth. "And God blessed them and said to them, 'Be fruitful and multiply and fill the earth'" (Genesis 1:28).

So here is the concern: loving parents baptize their babies for the remission of their sins just for being born when they did not need to be baptized, and it was the wrong form of baptism.

With that said, I hope this example helps.

Baptizing a baby that is innocent at birth is like buying a new, perfectly clean shirt from your favorite store and immediately washing it. But then, as the shirt has been worn for many years and needs to be washed, it isn't…it's still dirty. It means that we are still in our sins.

How many souls fit into this category? How many souls are dying to die with Jesus for the remission of their sins? How many souls are walking around with so many piled-up sins over the years, feeling guilty day by day and year after year?

Thank God for God! For He is longsuffering, not wishing that any should perish but that all should reach repentance (2 Peter 3:9).

Let us never forget what God had the apostle Peter write,

> In the days of Noah, while the ark was being prepared [for the flood] in which a few, that is, eight persons, were brought safely though water! Baptism, which corresponds to this, now saves you, not as a removal of dirt from the body but as an appeal to God for a good conscience through the resurrection of Jesus Christ.
>
> 1 Peter 3:20–21

Only eight people believed God when He said He was going to flood the earth. Now God asks for all to trust Him, not with a command to build an ark for many years but to allow your God-given conscience to lead you to obey with faith something that takes all of about two seconds, which is to die with Christ in baptism.

Can a baby believe the gospel, repent, or exercise faith?

I urge you to consider this for your soul's welfare because if you haven't submitted to the believer's death, door number 5 is what awaits you.

Doorway 5

> Christianity will go. It will vanish away and shrink. I needn't argue about that. I'm right, and I will be proved right. We're more popular than Jesus now. I don't know which will go first, rock 'n roll or Christianity. Jesus was alright, but His disciples were thick and ordinary. It's them twisting it that ruins it for me.
>
> —John Lennon

Here are some of the reasons for man's unbelief:

1. Pride: "Pride goes before destruction" (Proverbs 16:18).

Could it be that John Lennon's lyrics of the song "Imagine" are what was really going on in his heart when he wrote the song?

It's hard to imagine John Lennon finding it easy to think that heaven does not exist, that the sky is as far as we should go, and that each day seems to happen by chance. John and many like him, whether famous or not, must also convince themselves that hell can't be a real place either.

God tells us in the Bible what is going on in the minds of unbelievers: they are *suppressing the truth.*

"For the wrath of God is revealed from heaven against all ungodliness and unrighteousness of men, who by their unrighteousness suppress the truth. For what can be known about God is plain to them, because God has shown it to them" (Romans 1:18–19).

What has God shown man?

"For his invisible attributes, namely, his eternal power and divine nature, have been clearly perceived, ever since the creation of the world, in the things that have been made, *so they are without excuse*" (Romans 1:20, author's italics).

What God is saying here is that people suppress His truth, living lives that are unrighteous and ungodly, even though they know by what they see around them that God is real. That, my friend, is pride. How sad it is to think that John Lennon's words fit God's description.

"They did not honor him as God or give thanks to him but they became futile in their thinking and their foolish hearts were darkened" (Romans 1:21).

    2. *Almost Persuaded*: "King Agrippa replied to Paul, 'In a short time, will you persuade me to become a Christian?'"

(Acts 26:28).

John, a friend from New York, and I met for breakfast one morning. His life was spinning out of control. He was very successful in the finance world, but his marriage had spun out of control. He, like many, had certain spiritual baggage that had weighed on him all of his life. John owned the problems in his life and was ready to find out the truth of certain things. After he asked for a Bible, I asked him to go home and simply read the first chapter, Genesis.

We met a few weeks later for breakfast, and I asked him one question, "John, do you believe the first line in the Bible, 'In the beginning, God created the heavens and the earth'?"

He shook his head and answered, "No, I do not."

When I asked John where his late mother was, he answered, "Heaven," to which I replied, "How do you know that?"

He had no reply.

    3. *Family Tradition*: "But in vain do they worship me, teaching as doctrines the precepts of men" (Matthew 15:9).

A young fifteen-year-old golf student, Aaron, whom I have had the pleasure of teaching for a number of years, during one lesson, without warning, made this statement, "Mr. C., you know I'm Jewish, right?"

"Yes," I responded. What he said next was shocking.

"Mr. C., I believe that Moses existed but not that he parted the Red Sea with his staff."

I said to him next, "Aaron, it sounds like you don't believe in your own faith." While he thought about what he would say next, I asked him, "Aaron, can you tell me what happens to a person when they die?"

With incredible exasperation, he said, "That's the problem! There has to be more life!"

I agreed and then asked, "So where do we find it?"

He said, "I believe in reincarnation!"

I looked at Aaron and asked him if he knew of anyone who had been reincarnated, to which he shook his head, "No."

I said, "Aaron, it's not reincarnation that you need to know about. It's resurrection." Immediately, his head fell down as I mentioned the cross of Jesus Christ. Aaron didn't like my answer that day, but I pray that he will pick up the Bible and find out for himself.

4. *Lack of Knowledge*: "My people are destroyed for lack of knowledge" (Hosea 4:6).

Mike was another one of my long-standing golf students. He had a great job selling highly sophisticated medical equipment to doctors. He had a love for the game of golf and a good conversation. On more than one occasion, Mike would ask me about my political views. Sometimes, our conversations would carry over to the spiritual realm. Mike told me his belief one day, which is a very common view today, "Tom, when we die, we're just food for the worms."

I replied, "You're right; our bodies go in the ground, but our souls go back to God, who gave them."

"And the dust [body] returns to the earth as it was, and the spirit [soul] returns to God who gave it" (Ecclesiastes 12:7).

5. *Atheism*: "The fool has said in his heart, 'There is no God'" (Psalm 14:1).

One morning, I was setting up the room at the hotel where we typically have Sunday morning church services when the hotel manager walked in and introduced himself as Walker.

As he dusted me in speed, setting up all the chairs in perfect order, he suddenly said, "I appreciate what you do, and I've studied all the religions, but I don't believe in any of them." My response was, "Me neither!"

He looked at me funny and asked, "What do you mean?"

I replied, "It's not about religion. It's about Jesus Christ on the cross."

He responded, "That's what I meant; it includes what you are saying."

We had finished setting up together, and there was the right pause to ask him, "Walker, can you tell me what happens to you when you die?"

He said confidently, "When I die, I'll decide what I'm going to do next."

I replied, "I hope you don't take this the wrong way, but how can you? You're dead!"

Walker stood there frozen for a good five seconds before he said, "I never thought of it that way before!"

Here are five human beings who have their own real ideas as to what happens after death. If we asked the question to the 8.7 billion people in the world, "What happens to you when you die?" How many other answers might we get? Now, that is a viral moment!

John Lennon suppresses the truth! John from New York is in flat-out denial! Aaron, the golfer, wants to live!

Mike, the medical man, thinks you live, you die, and that's it!

Walker, the hotel manager, thinks he'll decide after he dies what he will do!

    6. *Doubt*: "Trust in the LORD with all your heart and do not lean on your own understanding" (Proverbs 3:5).

A Sad Song about Death and Doubting God:

If you listen to many songs on the radio, there are times when you can feel the actual pain and emotions of the singer. Perhaps never have we experienced it more than from singer-songwriter Gilbert O'Sullivan in his song "Alone Again (Naturally)." In it, he talks about both of his parents dying while at the same time being jilted at the altar, almost getting married. The overwhelming pain of it all causes him to tell the world through his lyrics that he doubts whether God really exists, yet if He does, he wonders why God seems to be so far away from him personally.

Mr. O'Sullivan isn't the first, nor will he ever be the last to feel this way. Many, including this writer, once felt deserted by God, feeling like I was on an island by myself. This is why it becomes so important to read the Bible. In the book of Acts, Chapter 17, the apostle Paul told the people that they "should seek God, in the hope that they might feel their way toward Him and find Him." Yet, He is actually not far from each one of us. What happens next is almost indescribable, but the layers of doubt begin to fall off one by one. I liken it to the scripture that says, "Humble yourselves in the presence of the Lord, and he will exalt you" (James 4:10).

Only God knows what was in Mr. O'Sullivan's heart when he wrote such an emotional song as this. But words matter. He mentions doubt: if God really does exist, he feels deserted. The pain in his lyrics and voice is apparent.

    7. *Love of Money*: "What does it profit a man if he gains the whole world and loses his soul?" (Mark 8:36).

Another form of the unbeliever's death is simply not taking the time to acknowledge God in their lives because they are ruled by a desire for money.

In the Bible, Jesus answers someone in the crowd who has inquired about His inheritance. Here is Jesus's response:

"Take care, and be on guard against all covetousness, for one's life does not consist in the abundance of his possessions" (Luke 12:15).

Jesus explains by using this parable:

> The land of a rich man produced plentifully, and he thought to himself, what shall I do, for I have nowhere to store my crops? And he said, "I will do this: I will tear down my barns and build larger ones, and there I will store all my grain and my goods. And I will say to my soul, Soul, you have ample goods laid up for many years; relax, eat, drink and be merry."

Luke 12:16–19

What Jesus is about to say is critical for so many souls who are looking at closed gates.

"But God said to him, 'Fool! This night your soul is required of you…'" (Luke 12:20).

God is saying that this type of man is foolish because he lacks good judgment by not living with the right aim or motive in life. His mistake is fatal.

While the desire to be rich continues to be lived out today by souls who are satisfied with this world's goods instead of the treasures of heaven, God sends His message to all who are rich that tonight you may die without considering the years of eternity and God as your judge.

8. *Problems with Authority*: "Jesus said, 'All authority has been given to me in heaven and on earth'" (Matthew 28:18).

There's a 1980s song by the duo Hall & Oates called "She's Gone" still played on the radio today; in it, Daryl Hall sings about how he feels bombarded by his father concerning how he should live his life. He sings about how his dad's lectures to him feel like a boring sermon. In addition, Daryl switches the theme to the idea of losing a girlfriend, so much so that he would pay the devil to replace her. One might think that it's no big deal when mentioning the devil, but we have to ask ourselves this: "If the devil doesn't really exist, then why do we speak about him at all? Could it be that, like all of us in the world, both Hall & Oates are indeed on the side of the devil, unaware that their souls are in a life-and-death struggle with the authority of Almighty God? Wouldn't we all agree that there seems to be a constant battle when it comes to yielding to someone's authority?"

Whether it's a silent stop sign at the street corner that we roll through, getting home a few minutes late past our parents' curfew time, or simply telling a friend, "Don't tell me what to do!" we like to be in charge of ourselves, our choices, and what we think about how we get to heaven. It is so easy to believe what we want to believe. But I can tell you, as someone who fought what you might be fighting right now, that it becomes increasingly clearer each time you read the Bible who is in charge.

Please listen to this verse from the apostle Paul, "For the word of the cross is foolishness to those who are perishing, but to us who are being saved it is the power of God" (1 Corinthians 1:18). The meaning is that man has always been fighting the authority of God when it comes to how a person gets to heaven. With love, may I say that, first of all, it is God who made heaven, and that should give our souls a clue as to who is in charge. Before you and I were ever born, God chose how man was going to be saved. It is by the cross of Jesus Christ. Sadly, everyone else will perish due to the problem of authority.

Please allow this next verse into your heart and soul. The apostle Paul is speaking to those who were worshiping an unknown God.

> Therefore having overlooked the times of ignorance, God is now declaring to men that all people everywhere should repent, because he has fixed a day in which He will judge the world in righteousness through a Man whom He has appointed, having furnished proof to all men by raising Him from the dead.
>
> Acts 17:30, 31

9. *Hypocrites*: "Woe to you [...] hypocrites, because you shut off the kingdom of heaven from people..." (Matthew 23:13).

When the group Crosby Stills and Nash were at the peak of their careers in the late '70s and all of the '80s, they wrote a song that I listened to many times growing up called "Cathedral":

In the chorus of the song, we are told that a man is yelling loudly to have the gates of the church where he is at opened so that he can get out of there as quickly as possible. The question we must ask is, "What would cause someone to want to leave so abruptly, and why would any singer write about such things?" *Well, one of the reasons why people don't attend church services or want to leave a church is the amount of so-called hypocrisy in the church itself.* Has that thought ever come to your mind before? Perhaps you see a friend or have parents who go to church on Sunday but curse like the world on Monday. That can be very discouraging, for sure.

I don't know if you have ever heard the song "Cathedral" before, but it's possible that knowing people who profess Christianity to you but whose walk seems to be the opposite has brought you into the hiding place where you question the very validity of Jesus Christ, His cross, and the church. At the same time, please hear this scripture from the Bible that sheds an important light:

"The god of this world [the devil] has blinded the minds of the unbelievers, to keep them from seeing the light of the gospel of the glory of Christ, who is the image of God" (2 Corinthians 4:4).

One of the devil's ways of keeping someone unbelieving in Jesus Christ is by having them look for a weak moment in a Christian's life when they sin and play the hypocrite. As a Christian preacher of God's Word, I've spoken to many individuals who have said just that: "The church is filled with hypocrites." If you're in this group, I certainly understand. There was a time when I thought the same exact things, even to the point of thinking that people in the church use religion as a crutch. It was only after I began reading the Bible for myself that the opposite view came into my mind. I began to believe that man's lack of belief in Jesus Christ is a crutch made of excuses, and I had many. I found out that even after becoming a Christian, I would still wrestle with sin for the rest of my life. I found out that Christians start out as "babes in Christ" and then continue to mature through the grace and knowledge of God, still sinning as we go. No, not with any joy and true spiritual desire to do so. But when we do sin after becoming a Christian, we can do what the apostle John says in one of his letters in the Bible: "If we confess our sins [written to Christians, not unbelievers], He is faithful and righteous to forgive us our sins and to cleanse us from all unrighteousness" (1 John 1:9).

I ask you this with the love of God in my heart: "Are you going to tell God on Judgment Day that the reason you didn't believe the truth about His Son Jesus Christ, the reason you didn't have your sins washed away in baptism by His blood and have the grace and knowledge of God through His Word lead you victoriously to heaven is someone else's sins?" We are talking about your soul here.

Please remember that Christians are *forgiven sinners.*

But all unbelievers who are not Christians are *unforgiven.*

I urge you, reader, to get out of this room as fast as you can because you are heading straight for door number 6.

DOOR 6

SPIRITUAL DEATH

"Then Death and Hades were thrown into the lake of fire. This is the second death, the lake of fire."

Revelation 20:14

Doorway 6

Do you remember the blockbuster movie *Ghost* from 1990 starring Patrick Swayze and Demi Moore?

I'll cut to the chase. In one scene toward the end of the movie, there is a series of horrific screams from the mouth of a man named Willie, the bad guy who killed Sam (played by Swayze). After being hit by a car, with his physical body dead, Willie is shown as his soul leaves his body and is dragged off by a group of gruesome dark demons.

If you saw the movie, the two worst parts of seeing him being escorted off were the judgmental sounds of these evil spirits and the look on Willie's face that says, "I'm about to experience the worst thing ever."

It's just a Hollywood movie, but Willie wasn't prepared for death.

Amanda Peet is crying out, wanting to know what happens after she dies. Each day, 155,000 people around the globe are playing out their ultimate *Jeopardy!* game, most likely shouting, "Dear God, my life and my soul are in jeopardy."

Were they ready? Are you?

From Death's perspective, it's like a game of hide and seek… Ready or not, here I come!

As everyone around the world speaks about hell day in and day out, does the world really believe in such a place?

Here are some of the phrases used around the globe as a part of our everyday speech:

There's not a chance in *hell*. What the *hell* are you doing? Maybe if *hell* freezes over!

He beat the *hell* out of that guy! There'll be *hell* to pay!

It hurts like *hell*!

There's no way in *hell* I'm going to forgive them! *Hell* yeah!

Come *hell* or high water. Give 'em *hell*!

What the *hell* was that? (One of my golf students said after a bad shot.) All *hell* broke loose!

I'm going to catch *hell* for this! I did it for the *hell* of it.

The road to *hell* is paved with good intentions. War is *hell*!

The worst phrase that has ever come out of a man's mouth, the one most full of venom and hate, is, "You go to *hell*!"

Have you heard of the book *I Hope They Serve Beer in Hell* by Tucker Max?

One review said, "Hilarious, shocking, and brazenly honest."

I can only imagine how many people have read the book and now think that "hell isn't so bad."

Mankind speaks about the devil, too! Is he real or just imagined?

The *devil*'s in the details. Playing *devil*'s advocate. Speak of the *devil*!

The *devil* made me do it. What the *devil* are you doing? You made a deal with the *devil*!

If you are older, how many times growing up did you hear the song "The Devil Went Down to Georgia?" Was it just a song, or do we believe that the devil is always looking for a soul to steal away from God? Let the apostle Peter tell us:

"Your adversary, the devil, prowls around like a roaring lion, seeking someone to devour" (1 Peter 5:8). And that was stated to Christians. The devil already has unbelievers because you just read that he (the devil) blinds the minds of unbelievers. That, my friend, is the essence of stealing a soul away from God.

Currently and still playing on the radio is a song from one of the most elite bands of all time, The Eagles, called "One of These Nights." Part of the song is about a man looking for the right woman. He is torn between wanting to have a woman who is in some way like a daughter of the devil (loose and provocative) and one who is wholesome to the point of being like an angel wearing white. It's a catchy song that we know by heart. Yes, by heart, I mean that the words have lodged deeply into our hearts. They sit in the hiding spot for sure. Words have the power to determine what we are going to believe about almost anything. When it comes to the spiritual realm, it's very much the same.

"The word of God is living and active and sharper than any two-edged sword, and piercing as far as the division of soul and spirit able to judge the thoughts and intentions of the heart" (Hebrews 4:12).

What I am hoping to convey to you is this: words from songs find their way in. The devil does not want the Word of God to find its way in. But when you read the Bible, it is so powerful it finds its way to your hiding spot and removes all doubts as to the validity of hell, the devil, God, heaven, and everything in between. Songs will always be tools to lift us up or bring us down. When it comes to the devil, we only have to open up the Bible and listen to our Lord and Savior, Jesus Christ, when He spoke to one of the religious groups of His day who did not believe that He was the Messiah.

"You are of your father the devil, and your will is to do your father's desires. He was a murderer from the beginning and has nothing to do with the truth because there is no truth in him. When he lies he speaks out of his own character, for he is a liar and the father of lies" (John 8:44).

And now He speaks about *hell*:

"If your right eye causes you to sin, tear it out and throw it away. For it is better that you lose one of your members than that your whole body be thrown into *hell*" (Matthew 5:29, author's italics).

Only GOATs

We always think of the GOATs as the ones who are the greatest in their respective fields. However, when it comes to the spiritual realm, being a GOAT means spending an eternity in *hell*.

I'm greatly concerned for Elon Musk. He is no doubt the "GOAT" of the EV market, but listen to what he had to say about hell:

"I'm okay with going to hell if that is indeed my destination since the vast majority of all humans ever born will be there" (Elon Musk).

Here Is What Jesus Says about GOATs

"Before him will be gathered all the nations, and he will separate people, one from another as a shepherd separates the sheep from the goats. And he will place the sheep on his right, but *the goats on the left*" (Matthew 25:32–33).

There it is to see—our earlier courtroom scene with mankind on the left of the Judge.

"I said to you that you would die in your sins, for unless you believe that I am He, you will die in your sins" (John 8:24).

What does that look like? Dying in your sins?

"Then he will say to those on the left, 'Depart from me, you cursed, into the eternal fire prepared for the devil and his angels'" (Matthew 25:41).

Here is the most sobering portion of Scripture to the human soul…that the apostle John saw and wrote,

> And I saw the dead, great and small, standing before the throne, and books were opened. Then another book was opened, which is the book of life. And the dead were judged by what was written in the books, according to what they had done. Death and Hades gave up the dead who were in them, and they were judged, each one of them, according to what they had done. Then Death and Hades were thrown into the lake of fire. This is the second death, the lake of fire. And if anyone's name was not found written in the book of life he was thrown into the lake of fire.
>
> Revelation 20:12–15

Jesus gives us a view of the truth of what happens after we die,

> "There was a rich man who was clothed in purple and fine linen and who feasted sumptuously every day. And at his gate was laid a poor man named Lazarus, covered with sores, who desired to be fed with what fell from the rich man's table.
>
> "The poor man died and was carried by the angels to Abraham's side. The rich man also died and was buried,

and in Hades being in torment, he lifted up his eyes and saw Abraham far off and Lazarus at his side. And he called out, 'Father Abraham, have mercy on me, and send Lazarus to dip the end of his finger in water and cool my tongue, for I am in anguish in this flame.'

Abraham responds a little later in the text:

"'He is comforted here, and you are in anguish. And besides all this, between us and you a great chasm has been fixed, in order that those who would pass from here to you may not be able, and none may cross from there to us.'

"'Then I beg you, father, to send him to my father's house, for I have five brothers, so that he may warn them, lest they also come into this place of torment.'"

Luke 16:19–28

There is *no* mention of "purgatory" in the Bible! Instead, we will know immediately after we die where our soul will go for all eternity.

One out of everyone dies! Only one of these two was saved!

One will have comforting peace for all eternity; the other will be in horrible torment that never ceases, so much so that he's begging for someone to go tell his brothers who were still living.

You are alive today. We both know that it won't be a movie or a song that determines if you will go to heaven; it's God's living Word that penetrates the heart. To one, it leads to humility, and to another, pride. In 1988, the band Mike and the Mechanics wrote a song called "The Living Years."

It's a song about a father and a son being estranged from one another during their lifetime. How many of us fall into this category? I did when I was only eight years old. There can be nothing worse than a broken home with no father there to guide us along the way. If you get the chance, please listen to the song because it takes us, the listener, down a similar path from a spiritual perspective. In the song, the son is in utter despair because one morning, without any notice, his father passes away. He's in terrible anguish because he never got the time to say things that would make things right between them. May I ask you, dear reader, this: Have you made things right with your heavenly Father?

DOOR 7

NO MORE DEATH

"He will wipe away every tear from their eyes, and death shall be no more, neither shall there be mourning, nor crying, nor pain any more, for the former things have passed away."

Revelation 21:4

Doorway 7

Listen to These Words That Jesus Spoke about Those Who Will Be Saved

"Come, you who are blessed by my Father, inherit the kingdom prepared for you from the foundation of the world" (Matthew 25:34).

"Blessed are the dead who die in the Lord from now on" (Revelation 14:13).

"Today you will be with me in paradise" (Luke 23:43).

The Shepherd gives us eternal life!

"I am the good shepherd. The good shepherd lays down his life for the sheep" (John 10:11).

Jesus presents us innocent to the Father!

"And you, who once were alienated and hostile in mind, doing evil deeds, he has now reconciled in his body of flesh by his death, in order to present you holy and blameless and above reproach before him" (Colossians 1:21–22).

Jesus promises to prepare a room for each one of us. God cannot lie!

> Let not your hearts be troubled. Believe in God, believe also in me. In my Father's house are many rooms. If it were not so, would I have told you that I go to prepare a place for you? And if I go and prepare a place for you, I will come again and will take you to myself, that where I am you may be also.
>
> John 14:1–3

Heaven is a perfect place!

"He will wipe away every tear from their eyes, and death shall be no more, neither shall there be mourning nor crying, nor pain anymore, for the former things have passed away!" (Revelation 21:4).

We will be like Jesus!

"Beloved, we are God's children now, and what we will be has not yet appeared; but we know that when he appears we shall be like him because we shall see him as he is" (1 John 3:2).

There will be no racism in heaven!

> A great multitude that no one could number, from every nation, from all tribes and peoples and languages, standing before the throne and before the Lamb, clothed in white robes, with palm branches in their hands, and crying out with a loud voice, "Salvation belongs to our God who sits on the throne, and to the Lamb!"
>
> Revelation 7:9–10

No sins in heaven!

"But as for the cowardly, the faithless, the detestable, as for murderers, the sexually immoral, sorcerers, idolaters and all liars, their portion will be in the lake that burns with fire and sulfur, which is the second death" (Revelation 21:8).

"But nothing unclean will ever enter it, nor anyone who does what is detestable or false, but only those who are written in the Lamb's book of life" (Revelation 21:27).

Christians in the Lamb's Book of Life, in heaven!

"I entreat Euodia and I entreat Syntyche to agree in the Lord, help these women who have labored side by side with me in the gospel […] whose names are in the book of life!" (Philippians 4:2, 3).

Do you recall the graphic "the right script"?

Those four dots represented the letters "U.R.E.S." to make the word "Scriptures" appear. But it's even better than that if you allow me to add a few more letters that connect the spiritual dots.

This is the *meaning of life!*

U.R.E.S.U.R.R.E.C.T.E.D. from the dead to live forever in heaven with God.

The purpose of life is to know God!

Jesus said it best, "He lifted up his eyes to heaven, and said:

'Father, the hour has come; glorify your Son that the Son may glorify you, since you have given him authority over all flesh, to give eternal life, that they know you the only true God, and Jesus Christ whom you have sent" (John 17:1–3).

We will praise God for who He is in heaven!

"No longer will there be anything accursed, but the throne of God and of the Lamb will be in it and his servants will worship him" (Revelation 22:3).

We will have no more fear in heaven!

"My sheep hear my voice, and I know them, and they follow me, I give them eternal life, and they will never perish, and no one will snatch them out of my hand" (John 10:27).

We will be with so many amazing people in heaven!

"And as for the resurrection from the dead, 'I am the God of Abraham, and the God of Isaac, and the God of Jacob.' […] He is not God of the dead, but of the living" (Matthew 22:32).

Abraham, Isaac, Jacob, King David; Mary, the mother of Jesus; Joseph, Moses, Noah and his family. Joshua, Ruth, Boaz, Sarah, Hannah, the Ethiopian eunuch, the repentant thief on the cross, Elijah, Isaiah, Jeremiah, Daniel, Elizabeth, John the Baptist! Paul, John, Peter, James, and Bartholomew, to name a few.

The 3,000 at Pentecost, Lazarus, Cornelius and family, Martha and Mary, coworkers with you, your neighbor, your friends, your family! Your spouse, children, mother, and father!

We will have some of the greatest conversations in heaven!

No one, while living on earth, has ever gotten to see the face of God.

"They will see his face!" (Revelation 22:4).

I would like to leave you with a line from my personal favorite song of all time: Led Zeppelin's "Stairway to Heaven." They said it best in their song, and God says it best in His Word. There are indeed only two paths that man travels on in his pursuit of searching for the truth about what happens to us when we die. Jesus calls them the "wide and narrow gates." Jesus cautions us to enter through the narrow one because it's the only way to heaven. That narrow gate is Jesus Himself. All other ways are known as the broad or wide gate that only leads to destruction (Matthew 7:13, 14).

Led Zeppelin's song reminds us that there is still time to change the road we are walking on. But better than that is what God said through the apostle Peter:

"The Lord is patient toward you, not wishing for any to perish but for all to come to repentance" (2 Peter 3:9).

The last thing Jesus Christ our Lord said before He died was, "It is finished!" (John 19:30).

God's plan to forgive man started in the beginning when He knew that man would sin against Him. Before the foundation of the world, God prepared a way and a promise to save all people so that they may join Him in heaven.

When Jesus said, "It is finished," He was saying the plan and the promise were completed.

God, in His love, allowed sinful man to kill His innocent Son on the cross to take your place. Now that you have heard the gospel, the choice is yours.

Door 3   +   Door 4   =   Door 7

Thank you for taking the time to read this book. I hope it has convinced you to pick up a Bible and read for yourself the incredible love that God has for us. "How great is that love?" you ask. "For God so loved the world that he gave His only Son, that whoever believes in him should not perish but have eternal life" (John 3:16).

Man's fear of death is replaced with freedom only through what God has done for us in Jesus Christ.

"That through death He might render powerless him who had the power of death, that is, the devil, and might free those who through fear of death were subject to slavery all their lives" (Hebrews 2:14, 15).

I hope that you will remember the song from earlier in this book. "Imagine" has been rewritten with new and encouraging lyrics that we hope would cause you to believe in God and the heaven that awaits you if you hear Him.

Please visit "imaginemediaworks.us" to view the music video.

When you see the real young lady who sings the song, along with the music video we've prepared to show the world, I pray that you will forward it to someone else.

Finally, it is my sincere desire that through God's providence working in all of us, this book gets into the hands of Amanda Peet.

—In Christ's love,
Tom
Tc.covino@gmail.com

Bonus on the Next Page

You have to read the incredible truth of what happened to my brother in Christ and the illustrator of this book, Jason Roberts. It will leave you speechless and wanting to pick up the Bible and see for yourself…

A Word from the Illustrator, Jason Roberts

My life journey has been a strange odyssey, and now, as I am at the beginning of my seventh decade, I see God's hand in so many details of my life over the years and how He used circumstances to bring me to Him.

I grew up in a very religious family; we never missed going to church and often went to midweek services and other special occasions. But although my stepfather was very dedicated to being in church, there was very little church in him. There simply was no reality of the presence of Christ in our home. Beyond the oppressive religious environment, I experienced severe physical abuse in my childhood—my life was a constant terror of never knowing when he would explode into one of his tirades, which usually got taken out on me. I certainly did things that were wrong and needed to be corrected, but there is a quantum leap difference between correcting a child and simply using a child as the target for one's anger and frustration in ways that, if these things happened in more current times, they would have resulted in charges for assault.

In this religious, abusive, and rigid upbringing, I never knew if I was going to heaven or hell. An event happened when I was about twelve years old; I was about to be "confirmed" in a religious ceremony, but I was in a state of "mortal sin" at the time. I had sampled a bit of icing on a cake just before going to church and receiving Communion. Back in those days, you had to wait a certain amount of time after eating any solid food before receiving Communion. The prescribed minimum time had not yet elapsed before I partook of the Communion; sadly, I walked down the aisle to receive the wafer. I was too terrified to do anything else in the presence of my stepfather but what was normally expected of me…so as the wafer was placed on my tongue, I thought for sure I was on my way to hell.

For some reason, I just couldn't go to confession and get this dark blot removed from my soul and get back on the path to heaven; maybe I was too embarrassed, I'm not sure. So I just continued as before, acting as if nothing was wrong on the outside—I was singing in the choir and serving as an altar boy, but on the inside, I was in a state of terror, thinking I was in danger of hellfire. So, when the day came for me to partake of the sacrament of confirmation, I was in a state of "mortal sin" because of my cake-icing-tasting episode. At the last minute, just as we were lining up, I couldn't take it anymore. I bolted from the line and ran to the nearest confessional as fast as I could to remove the mortal sin from my soul. But just before I got there, I ran into my stepfather, who growled at me something like, "Where do you think you're going?" I told him I was going to confession. He said if I hadn't already gone, it was too late now, and he told me to "get back in line." As I was scared of my stepfather, I meekly obeyed. I got back in line, and with the other boys and girls, as they walked forward and one by one received the rite of confirmation, I also did the same, trembling within at the prospect of the spiritual consequences this would incur.

After the confirmation service was over, I thought to myself, *Oh boy, I have really done it to myself. I received a sacrament in a state of mortal sin!* I believed I had nested a mortal sin within a mortal sin, and now there was no way out…I was doomed to hell for sure now…all because of a little taste of some icing on a cake on the way to church.

It probably seems really silly as I relay this story to you, but for me, it was a heavy cloud over my head from about year twelve to year eighteen of my life. I thought I was doomed with no hope and, at the same time, was in a church culture that was religious without Christ—nothing in my church experience truly evidenced the love of God. Still, even in my young teen years, as clueless in general as I was, I discerned a lot of religiosity and hypocrisy constantly around me. The result was that when I finally left home at age eighteen to go to college, I threw it all out the window! I was finally free! Free of the guilt, free of the fear, free of the repression from my stepfather, and free of the dread I always carried around that I was going to hell with no hope of escape. At this point in my life, I declared myself to be an atheist.

I thought I was free, but I soon began to realize I really wasn't. Growing up with the abuse of my stepfather, the one thing that kept me going was my hatred for him and my desire to someday have revenge. I would fantasize about the day that I would be big enough and strong enough to do to him the things he did to me. So even though I was no longer under his thumb, in a sense, he still controlled me because my hatred and passion for revenge was like a cancer eating away at me from the inside…and I had no control over it. I was in complete bondage to it. As a result, I hated him even more because, although I was no longer under his direct control, he still controlled me by the emotional bondage that held me prisoner…and there was nothing within my power that I could do to get free.

After leaving college, I moved to New York in search of a career in show business. Shortly after moving to the "Big Apple," I started seeing a therapist; I so desperately wanted to be set free. After several months, my therapist was able to pinpoint my specific problem, but there really was no answer…and there was no power in the resources my therapist had that could set me free.

It was during this time that I began to seek spiritual answers. My atheism grudgingly gave way to agnosticism. As I thought about the order and design of nature and the universe, I thought to myself, *All this had to come from somewhere; it couldn't just all pop into existence from nowhere; after all, anything times zero is still just zero. So, there has to be a source of origin.* I just didn't know what it was, so I began to identify myself as an agnostic, and I began to search for spiritual truth. I read about Buddhism, and I checked out Scientology (in their program, they promised freedom if you paid them a whole bunch of money—in my heart, I felt like if you really had something as priceless as the power to truly set you free from your inner bondages, it would never be something with a price tag on it). I really got into New Age theosophy… but in all of this, my soul was still crying out to be set free (and if you knew me then, you would never have known this cauldron of emotion was boiling on the inside).

For all my searching, I still did not know why I was on planet earth and the answer to the big question, "What will happen when I die?" I used to muse to myself, *What would be worse, going to hell and being forever lost without hope yet still retaining my conscious awareness or simply ceasing to exist?* I would go back and forth on that one and never arrive at an answer since either possibility was too horrible to contemplate, and I was sure one of those two options was to be my fate. I came to the conclusion that if I ceased to exist when I died, it would be no different than if I never lived. So why wait? Why not just get it over with? Why wait until death took me? Staring at death in the face, I reeled back from the precipice of the chasm of eternity in stark terror. I couldn't face the reality of the conclusion that logical thinking led me to. So, even realizing that it was a logical conclusion, actually acting out the conclusion of my thinking was just too scary. I thought to myself, *Even though I may cease to exist when I draw my last breath, and it will be for me as though I had never been…what the heck, I'm enjoying life for the present*, and I chose to shut my eyes to the sure fate that awaited me in the future.

Living in New York, I was a young man in my prime, living the "Bohemian" artsy lifestyle. I freelanced as an illustrator and publishing production artist. I was also seeking to earn a living in the performing arts. I was having fun, doing my thing, yet still, deep down inside, I was still in bondage to the cancer of needing revenge for the abuses of my childhood, and I was still deeply troubled about not knowing what would happen to me after death. At times, it was as if I could sense a voice deep down in my spirit saying, "Hey, you're going to die someday; what are you going to do about it?" I kept trying to silence the voice; I did not want to think about it. But the voice never left me; it simply would not leave me in peace.

As I was pursuing jobs in show business, there were a couple of shows that I was in that were very interesting and unusual. One was a Broadway show called *Jumpers* by Tom Stoppard. The essence of the show is built around a series of monologues where the main character, a philosophy professor, is trying to figure out where everything came from. What is the point of origin of the universe? He never really did come to an answer for all his questions, but it sure was interesting in the many ways and examples he posed the questions. It got me thinking about it also… actually, I thought about it a lot.

Another Show was *Sergeant Pepper's Lonely Heart Club Band on the Road*. Actually, this was really a rock opera that loosely followed a storyline similar to Goethe's *Faust*. In the story of the rock opera, Billy Shears is tempted to sell his soul to the devil in order to realize his dream of being a rock star. Songs from various Beatles albums (especially Sergeant Pepper) were tied together in such a way as to create the storyline. Hmmmm, heaven, hell, the devil…interesting…it got me thinking. Funny story: after opening night at the Beacon Theatre on Upper Broadway, there was a cast party. John Lennon happened to be there at the party; unbeknownst to me, a reporter snapped a quick photo of John Lennon with Robert Stigwood, producer; Leee Childers, publicist; and Bruce Scott, star of the show. Except it wasn't actually Bruce Scott standing there; it was me. So I had my picture in the paper the next day with John Lennon (the paper mistakenly identified me as Bruce Scott, but anyway, at least I got my picture in the paper with a living legend—*see the photo below)*.

November 1974, from left to right: Jason Roberts, Hammeroid; Lee Childers, Publicist; Robert Stigwood, Producer; John Lennon

So, for several years, I was doing my thing in New York and having a lot of fun at it. Yet still, on the inside, I was in bondage to my inner demons of resentment, and I was still searching for an answer to the question that continually plagued me: "What happens after I die?"

As I continued my fruitless quest for the answer to the biggest question we all face, in 1975, I was having a discussion with a fellow highly accomplished performer friend who happened to be a Christian. I could never understand why such a talented and intelligent person believed in something that, to me, seemed ridiculous, but he was really into the "Jesus Thing," which was cool with me as long as he didn't push it on me. We were talking, and the conversation started to veer into a serious and personal direction and delved into spiritual issues. At one point, he asked me, "Do you believe in Jesus?" My immediate inner thought was, *Of course not; I'm not into any of that religious stuff.* (I had more than my fill with legalistic religion growing up, and although I was seeking truth in a myriad of directions, as far as I was concerned, Jesus was off the table for consideration because my mind had become so tainted against Jesus as a result of what I experienced growing up.) I was about to say "No" to his question, but as the word was on my lips, in my spirit, in vivid clarity came a voice saying, "Don't deny Me because you don't know." I sat in stunned silence for a moment and then said, "I don't know." At that moment, it was as if the darkness in my soul was infused with light, and I knew in my heart of hearts that Jesus was real and He could save me from my greatest fear, the fear of death. I didn't know much of anything at that point; I did not really know the message of the gospel (even after years of catechism). I just somehow knew in the deepest part of my being that if I put my trust in Christ, I no longer need to fear what would happen on the day I left my life in this world. I actually felt as if I had been "born again," although I did not know this was actually in the Bible; if I were to put words to my experience, that was what came to my mind. It was more than just the answer to my questions; I experienced the Spirit of God coming into my spirit, invading the darkness of my soul with His light and life.

 This was 1975. The next few years were spent delving into the Bible to find out what this "Jesus Thing" was all about. As of this writing (February 2023), that was forty-eight years ago. What happened after that is another story, but I do want to mention one significant thing: as I began reading the Bible and was meditating on the teachings of Jesus, I came across a section that talked about forgiveness. I felt in my spirit that God was instructing me to forgive my stepfather. My heart rebelled against this. I dug in my heels against what the scripture taught and vehemently thought, *No, no way! He doesn't deserve to be forgiven; he deserves to be punished...I can't forgive him; I want him to pay for what he did to me!* But in my spirit, I felt the Spirit of God gently nudge me, saying, "Do *you* deserve to be forgiven?" Reluctantly in my heart, I cried out, "God, I don't feel like doing this, but I choose to obey Your Word." At the moment of the submission of my will to His, I felt a tsunami of the love of God sweep through my soul, sweeping out the rot and corruption of hatred and the need for revenge. I was finally free of the insidious cancer of the soul that was eating me alive from the inside out and that held me in bondage. I was finally set truly free by the power of God—Him doing what He alone can do.

Since that day, I have continued walking with Christ day by day. I know that He, and He alone, is the answer to man's deepest questions: "Why am I here? What happens to me after I die? How shall I live while I am in this world?"

A few years later, after I moved to Los Angeles, as I was endeavoring to walk with Christ and grow in the Spirit, it suddenly hit me: I realized that I had never been baptized correctly or, as the scriptures teach, immersed in water. Like many, I had been sprinkled as a child, so I really didn't think much about it. But one day, I woke up with an overwhelming conviction that I needed to be baptized as soon as possible in obedience to the command of Christ. I felt such a strong urgency about the matter (I believe this was the conviction of the Holy Spirit). I made immediate arrangements to be baptized at the church I was attending.

I was so happy when the day finally arrived, and I felt a huge sense of relief when I came back up and out of the water. After that, I experienced a lifting of inner burdens I was carrying and, I think, the blessing of the Lord that comes with obedience from the heart.

Fast forward to the present: when I met Tom Covino and was invited to collaborate on this project, I jumped at the chance. My desire is to lead a life that is honoring to God and to share the good news of eternal life that is in Christ with as many as will listen. This book was an opportunity to get this message out to a hurting world in need of answers to the deep heart questions and to introduce them to the One with those answers and the power to live as we were created to live for today.

Is the message true? I implore you to search for yourself and examine the evidence. The resurrection of Christ from the dead has more than ample evidence to convince anyone with an open heart of the reality of this event if they examine the facts for themselves. The amazing record of prophecies in the Bible is such a powerful fact to consider: details about Christ were foretold in advance, where He would be born, when He would publicly present Himself as the Messiah, the King of Israel, His crucifixion and the resurrection—all foretold in advance hundreds of years before Christ. And on and on it goes; the facts are so staggering that a plethora of books are written about this.

To sum up, "Once I was lost, now I am found." The lost and wounded child has been healed, and now I know the answers to the deep questions that I desperately sought. My hope for you, dear reader, is that you will hear the voice of the Son of God who said, "Truly, truly, I say to you, whoever hears my word and believes him who sent me has eternal life. He does not come into judgment, but has passed from death to life" (John 5:24).

—Jason Roberts
San Antonio, Texas
March 12, 2023